Alexander Pirie

**A Dissertation on Baptism**

Intended to illustrate the origin, history, design, mode, and subjects, of that sacred institution: wherein the mistakes of the Quakers and Baptists on that subject are pointed out. Vol. 1

Alexander Pirie

**A Dissertation on Baptism**

*Intended to illustrate the origin, history, design, mode, and subjects, of that sacred institution: wherein the mistakes of the Quakers and Baptists on that subject are pointed out. Vol. 1*

ISBN/EAN: 9783337410803

Printed in Europe, USA, Canada, Australia, Japan

Cover: Foto ©Lupo / pixelio.de

More available books at **www.hansebooks.com**

A
# DISSERTATION
ON
# BAPTISM,

INTENDED

To illuſtrate the Origin, Hiſtory, Deſign, Mode and Subjects of that Sacred Inſtitution:

WHEREIN

The Miſtakes of the Quakers and Baptiſts on that ſubject are pointed out, and their objections refuted:

TO WHICH IS ADDED

An Enquiry into the Lawfulneſs of Eating Blood.

---

By ALEXANDER PIRIE,
Minister of the Gospel at NEWBURGH.

---

PERTH:
Printed for the Author.
M,DCC.LXXXVI.

# PREFACE.

MANY of my religious acquaintances, when conversing with me on the subject of baptism, have expressed a doubt of the divine authority for administring that institution to infants; so that if they continue the practice it is only because, in a dubious case, they reckon it best to err on the safe side. My own mind, too, had long considered this subject as a matter of doubtful disputation. Suspense, always accompanied with anxiety, is a disagreeable state of mind in every case; but it is particularly so, when its object is of a religious kind. Faith in the divine appointment of an institution can alone render the observation of it a part of religious service; since "whatsoever is not of faith is sin." Suspense in a matter of this kind, then, must not only fill the mind with anxiety, but mar that satisfaction of heart, which results from a consciousness of obeying Jesus, by observing the things which he commands. This consideration induced me to examine the scriptures relating to this point with attention, relying on the promise---" If any man incline to do his will, he shall " know the doctrine, whether it be of God." The result of these inquiries is now offered to the view of the public; and if it shall tend to illustrate the truth, or establish the mind of the Christian in a matter of so great importance, the Publication will not be in vain.

Of late years the Baptists have published again and again in support of their argument, and now seem to boast as if their cause had obtained a decided victory, while the silence of their opponents seems to admit the claim. Comparing their arguments, however, with scripture, I began to suspect them more plausible than solid. This determined me to publish my views of that subject: yet not chusing to enter the field as a disputant, I have arranged my ideas in the form of a Dissertation; in a doctrinal rather than a controversial manner,---only making some animadversions on the opinions of the Quakers and Baptists as they occurred, and seemed to cross my sentiments.

This work, then, is not intended as a direct answer to any particular writer. I indeed have taken a variety of quotations from Mr M'Lean's writings; but it is only because I consider his works as containing all that has been said on his side of the question, and that with perspicuity and elegance. The pamphlet I refer to is entitled "A Defence of Believer Baptism," published in answer to an anonymous author at Glasgow: and my reader is desired to observe, that to avoid too frequent references to the particular pages of that work, the whole that I have quoted from it on the mode of Baptism is to be found betwixt p. 55 and 65 of the foresaid performance.

The more I attend to this Gentleman's writings, the more I am persuaded that his misconceptions on

the

the head of Baptism originate in false ideas of some very leading points of revealed truth. He seems to be much mistaken in his notions concerning the difference between the churches of the old and new testaments, the two covenants and the two seeds of Abraham; as also concerning both circumcision and baptism. To detect his mistake in articles of so great importance I have committed to writing a considerable number of thoughts, which I intend soon to publish, provided the following dissertation shall meet the approbation of the public.

The plan of this dissertation at least is *new:* and as the force of evidence resulting from an argument depends much on a proper arrangement of its parts, I have endeavoured to collect the rays of evidence into one common point, so as to produce the most forcible impression on the mind. How far I have succeeded must be left to the public determination.

With respect to my thoughts on the eating of blood, I shall only say, that two motives have determined their publication---a deep conviction of the importance of the subject, to men in general and to christians in particular; and a desire to recall the public attention to a point too generally reckoned of trifling import, though meriting a more serious discussion. Possessed of this idea, the writer has investigated the subject at a considerable length; and he only begs to be read with attention, and judged with impartiality.

NEWBURGH, July 21, 1786.

# A DISSERTATION ON BAPTISM.

## SECT. I.

### On Baptism *in general*.

THE application of water to the body for the purpose of health and cleanliness, is a practice founded in nature, and has been in use among men from the beginning. We find also infinite wisdom, from the earliest period, has chosen water, and its application to the body as symbols of the divine spirit, and the application of his influences to the mind, for the purposes, of spiritual health and purity. No symbol has a more obvious foundation in nature.

This religious use of water is the thing that is principally called Baptism. That water was the symbol of the spirit is evident from scripture. To pour water on men and to pour the spirit on them are every where synonimous expressions. When Jesus spoke of the spirit he called him " living water." So early as the days of Jacob, water was applied to the body as a figure of that purity of mind, which is necessary in the service of God. Thus when Jacob was about to go up to Bethel to erect an altar to Jehovah, he " said to his household, " Be *clean*, and change your garments; and let " us arise and go up to Bethel." Gen. xxxv. 1, 2, 3. This was nothing new: it was but a specimen of the practice of the church from the entrance of sin. The same mystical use of water has been continued in all the dispensations of religion. Not only the Jews, but the heathens, in all their various forms of religion, carefully observed their lustrations and purifications, when approaching their God. The laver stood near the altar in the house of Jehovah, and at the entrance to the holy place: and even in Britain our Druids, the heathen priests of antiquity, so exactly retained the ancient institution, that we no where find one of their altars for sacrifice, but we find at the same time

time a fountain or rivulet of water in its neighbourhood. So early and so universal was this religious use of water; and so exactly can an external ceremony of religion be maintained, while the spiritual intention of it is almost entirely lost.

To the water, religion has added the application of oil and blood. The oil, which was used in this religious application to the body, was called holy oil. The blood was always that of a sacrifice, all of which were dedicated to God and thus were considered holy. These were applied to the bodies of all, who were initiated into the service of God. Kings and prophets were anointed with the holy oil. No priest could draw nigh to minister in the tabernacle of Jehovah, until he was first washen in water, anointed with oil and had blood put upon him, even the blood of consecration. Lev. viii. 6, 12, 23, 24. In the same chapter we are told, that Moses sprinkled the altar and all his vessels both with blood and oil, in consecrating them to the divine service. The tabernacle was sanctified in the same manner, ver. 10. In short, " almost all things are by the " law purged with blood;" nor was the application of oil less extensive. "Moses took the anointing oil, and anointed the tabernacle and all therein, and sanctified them."

These three materials used in Baptisms, or religious initiations into the service of Jehovah, were all symbolical of the several Influences of the Holy Spirit. The water expressed that purity of heart the spirit confers; the oil by its softning and lenient effects, was calculated to represent love, mercy, peace and joy—all the fruits of the spirit. Blood was the symbol of pardon and forgiveness, as it was always shed for the remission of sin.

John says "There are three that bear witness on earth, the spirit, the water and the blood." 1. Ep. v. 8. The spirit is the same as the oil, with which, he says, all Christians are anointed; chap. ii. 20, 27. "Ye have an anointing from the holy one—the anointing which ye have received of him abides in you." This same anointing, he adds, is a true witness; "is truth and is no lie." Consequently the oil in these verses is the same as the spirit in the 8th verse of the fifth chapter: and thus John's three witnesses will be found to have been always on earth; connected with a profession of faith in the divine record, and attesting this great truth, "That God has gi-"ven to us eternal life and this life is in the "Son," whose atoning and vital influences have been always visibly expressed by these witnesses.

We have seen how they did bear witness, during the patriarchal and mosaic dispensations. As access to God, pardon, purity and life could only be obtained by these three; these solemnly attested this truth, that all the blessings mentioned could be only obtained through the Son, whose types they were. So clearly did they attest the truth of the record of God, that he has given us eternal life in his Son. The same three bore witness to the Son, when he tabernacled among us in person. Before he entered upon his public ministry, he was baptized with water in Jordan; immediately after which he was anointed with the Holy Spirit above measure. With the holy oil the Father anointed him to be king over Zion. After all he had still another baptism to be baptized with, even that with his own blood, before he could enter into the holy place, there to appear in the presence of God for us. Thus water, oil, and blood

blood gave testimony concerning the Son of God while on earth. After he ascended, the same three continued to bear testimony to the truth of the Gospel. The water in Baptism, the anointing abiding in the Christian, and the cup of the blood of the New Testament, continue still in the church of Christ Jesus. Two of these, the water and the blood, are visible to the eye of the body; the other, the anointing or holy oil, is visible too in its effects on the life of the Christian. The very word *Christian* signifies the anointed. In the days of the Apostles, oil was literally applied for religious purposes. Not only the Apostles themselves "a-" "nointed with oil many that were sick, and " healed them," (Mark vi. 13.) but James says, " Is any sick among you? let him call for the " elders of the church; and let them pray o-" ver him, anointing him with oil in the name " of the Lord:" not that he may die, as the papists conceive; but that the sick may be raised up, and his sins may be forgiven him. James v. 15, 16.

Thus Baptism in general consisted in a religious application of a fluid to the body, as a solemn initiation into the service of God. We

have

have seen what fluids were employed in this ceremony, let us now attend to.,

## SECT. II.

The MANNER of their APPLICATION.

Water, oil and blood, though all applied to the body for religious purposes, yet have been applied in very various modes. Persons and things are said sometimes to have been washen with water; which includes both *immersion* or dipping and *rinsing*, since one may be washen in either of these ways. Sometimes they *bathed* their flesh in water; which might be done two ways; either by applying water to the body as in fomentation, or by putting the body among the water. At other times we read of *sprinkling* with water.

In the law of Moses we no where read of the rites of initiation being performed by immersion. When Moses brought Aaron and his sons to the door of the tabernacle, to sanctify them, that they might minister to the Lord in the priest's office, he washed them with water; but it is not said whether by immersion or rinsing. It is most probable, that the last mode was used on on this occasion, as the bodies of Aaron and his sons could not be kept so long under water, as was necessary to wash or cleanse them. Simple dipping is not washing at all. A thing may be washen without dipping it, but dipping without rinsing can wash nothing.

‘ With respect to the oil and blood, they also were variously applied. We have specimens of all these different modes of application in the 8th chapter of Leviticus. The altar was anointed by *sprinkling;* but Aaron and his sons by *pouring out* the oil on their heads, ver. 11, 12. The blood was applied by *sprinkling*, as in ver. 19. or by putting it with the finger upon the part to be sanctified, as in ver. 15, 23, 24. In this last manner, the oil was also sometimes applied, as in cleansing the leper, Lev. xiv. 28. ’

It may be observed, that these religious applications of a fluid under the law, were intended, either as a sign of initiation into the fellowship of the church with her God, or into some sacred office in her; or, lastly, of a restoration or re-admission into her fellowship. The cleansing of the leper is an instance of the last of these, as in Lev. 13 and 14 chapters. The leper had been a member of the church formerly,

ly, but was cast out because of this uncleaness; and before he can be re-admitted to her fellowship; he must be sanctified or cleansed by water, oil and blood, applied in all the different modes used in the consecration or initiation of the priests.

All these modes of applying liquids to the body are called by Paul *Baptisms*, Heb. ix. 10. It is well known that the word rendered *washings* in that verse is in the Greek, Baptisms, the same as purifications. He is here giving a summary of the ritual services, in which the application of fluids to the body is one of the most considerable. And that all the various purifications prescribed by the law are included in this, must be evident to every man of discernment. If it means only immersion, then the Apostle leaves out of his account by far the greater number of modes of purification prescribed by the law; which is very unlike his usual accuracy. But the context determines the point beyond a rational doubt; as he proceeds immediately to give instances of these Baptisms —" If the blood of bulls and goats, and the " ashes of an heifer, *sprinkling* the unclean, sanc-" tifieth to the purifying of the flesh. Moses,
" with

"with water, scarlet-wool and hysop, *sprinkled* both the book and all the people."

How properly are these called " divers Baptisms!" different materials or liquids were employed in them, as we have already seen; diverse instruments were used, as the hand, wool, hysop; and all were applied in very various manners as is also shewen.

That sprinkling is to be classed among these diverse Baptisms is certain. The priest of the law could not enter the Holy place, till the sacrifice was slain, and its blood sprinkled upon himself and his garments, to sanctifie himself and his garments with him, Lev. viii. 30. This was fulfilled in Jesus Christ, as Paul assures us, who could not enter heaven, till he entered in his own blood. He is our Priest and sacrifice. Sprinkled with his own blood he had a right to enter heaven, and to sanctify the people, or to apply to them the blood of sprinkling that they might be made priests to God; as Aaron's sons were sanctified at the same time with himself by the same blood of sprinkling. Speaking of this act as performed in himself, he expressly calls it *Baptism*. Luke xii. 50. " I have a " Baptism to be Baptized with, and how am I
" straitened

" ſtraitened till it be accompliſhed." To underſtand this clearly we muſt obſerve, that as Aaron was firſt baptized with water, then with oil, and finally with blood, after which he was fully conſecrated; ſo Jeſus was firſt baptized with water, then with the ſpirit, the holy oil; and now, ſays he, I am anxious to have my laſt baptiſm performed, which muſt be by my own blood. He was only made *perfect* by ſufferings. This finiſhed his conſecration.

To tell us, that this is only a figure, to repreſent the greatneſs of his ſufferings, even as they are ſet forth in Old Teſtament metaphors, by his ſinking in deep mire, and coming into deep waters, where the floods overflow him,—is to interpret ſcripture inconſiſtently.

Every body knows, that ſinking in deep waters, and coming into overflowing floods, mean great afflictions; but where ſhall we find Baptiſm uſed in any ſuch ſenſe? Even where it is uſed metaphorically, it always ſignifies initiation, as this is its obvious deſign, but never ſuffering of any kind, much leſs the greatneſs of ſuffering.* Our Lord's Baptiſm with blood was indeed

* I know it will be objected that ſufferings are called *Baptiſm*, when our Lord ſays to the ſons of Zebedee.—" Ye
" ſhall

deed connected with suffering; in the same manner as the Baptism of the high-priest was connected with the sufferings of the sacrifical ram. But the sufferings of the ram of consecration were not Baptism; but the sprinkling of

"shall drink of my cup, and be baptized with the bap-"tism that I am baptized with." Matt. xx. 23. to understand these words we must observe that they are an answer to a petition presented by these two disciples, desiring admission to the dignified office of chief ministers in their master's kingdom. To this request our Lord replies by pointing out the *initiatory* services, which must be submitted to by candidates for so high an office——Ere you can enter to so high offices in my kingdom you must drink of my cup, and be baptized with my baptism, or pass through the introductory sufferings. Baptism, then in this passage, still denotes *initiation* to a society or office. It is connected with sufferings, indeed, but the sufferings are called Baptism, not with respect to their *nature*, but with regard to their *design*. "Ought not Christ to have suffered "these things, and to *enter into* his glory." The idea of Baptism and the idea of suffering are totally distinct.

It may be added, that in this passage there is no reference to *plunging* at all, but to the mode of initiating a prophet, priest or king into his office according to the law; which was never performed by *immersion* but by *anointing*. It particularly refers to the last Baptism of the priest, when he was *sprinkled* with the blood of the ram of consecration, which perfected his initiatory service. At any rate then this passage avails the Baptists nothing.

of his blood on the priest was so. In like manner, the sprinkling of the blood of Jesus, the consequence of his sufferings, and the finishing part of his consecration, was his baptism, which he was pained to have accomplished, knowing what he must suffer in his way to it.

It may be added, that Paul expresses the Baptism of Christians by *sprinkling* and *washing*, Heb. x. 22. " Having your hearts sprinkled " from an evil conscience," by the inward baptism of his holy spirit, " and your bodies washed " with pure water" in the external institution of baptism. Moreover, as the oil was poured upon the heads of the initiated under the law, so the Holy Ghost is said to be poured out on the Christians: And what is called *pouring out* in Acts x. 45. is expresly called *Baptizing* in Acts xi. 16. So evident is it that sprinkling, washing, pouring upon, anointing, are all Scripture Baptisms.

## SECT. III.

### *The Word* BAPTISM.

That *Immersion* is the primary idea of the Greek word *Baptisma* or *Baptismos* seems to be

B

a miftake. This word is originally derived from *bapto*, the leading idea of which in all Greek writers is *dyeing*, giving a new *tincture* or *colour* to any thing. In its derivatives, it denotes dyers, the art of dyeing, dye-houfes. Now as the art of dyeing is generally practifed by immerfion or dipping, hence the word came to fignifie alfo dipping or plunging.

Keeping this in view, we may eafily get at the reafon why the Scripture inftitutions for initiation into the church or her offices were called Baptifm; and particularly why the initiating ordinance of Chriftianity is fo called. By initiation into a fociety or office we take on a new tincture or dye, or a new character, and even a new name. It was fo in the Old Teftament: it is particularly fo in the New. Now as this is the defign and meaning of Chriftian Baptifm; as it is intended to exprefs our putting on the Lord Jefus Chrift, the new man, a new character indeed, no word could be found more proper for expreffing this idea. Befides, as Baptifm in Greek fignifies alfo immerfion or dipping, which is the moft full and perfect application of water or any liquid to the body, or thing dipped, when an ordinance confifts in an

application

application of a fluid to the body, it was obviously proper to call it by a name, which denotes the most perfect act of the kind. Yet to infer from this, that no mode of applying a liqu'd to the body, save dipping alone, can be called Baptism, is not fair since we have the clearest evidence to the contrary. The motion of a ship or boat on the water is called in our language *sailing*, which in its most proper sense denotes motion by means of a sail. Yet it is well known that a boat can be moved on the water by oars or even by the current, without a sail at all. How absurd then would it be to argue that none of these last mentioned modes of passing by water are included in the idea of sailing; because sailing in a strict sense signifies passing by water by means of a sail? Yet this is no more absurd than the argument of the Baptists, That men can no more be baptized by *sprinkling* or *pouring*, than they can eat the Lord's Supper by *seeing* or *smelling;* because, forsooth, Baptism principally means dipping.

This idea may be illustrated a little further. A physician directs his patient to take a sail on the water daily. A man of plain sense, on reading this direction, would instantly conclude, that if the patient was conveyed by water, whether by the current, wind, oar or sail, the docter's intention was fulfilled. No; says a critic, the word sailing in the English language, in its most obvious signification, denotes motion by a sail. A man can no more be said to sail with an oar, than to fly with a staff. Had the doctor intended motion on water by an oar, he would have used the word *rowing;* the proper English word for expressing that idea.—Thus the plainest direction in the world, by the dint of criticism, could be rendered so intricate, that no man of plain understanding could possibly unravel it. The patient may die, ere the dispute be determined.

The truth is, Baptism is not so called from its mode of application, but from its design or intention, to point out our being washen from sin, and putting on a new tincture or character. It says, in other words, be clean, and change your garments; and *rise* and go up to Bethel the house of God. It may be further observed, that,

As Baptism is a sign of admission into a church, it is used in scripture to denote *initiation* in general, in whatever manner the fluid be applied;

ed; yea, when there is no application of a fluid at all. Thus Israel are said to have been Baptized, *i. e.* initiated into the system of Moses, in the cloud and in the sea. The cloud and water were both employed in this service; yet neither of them were in immediate contact with the bodies of the Israelites.

## SECT. IV.

### *The Jewish* Baptisms.

We have already seen, that all who were admitted into sacred offices in the Mosaic tabernacle, were initiated to these offices by a threefold Baptism by water, blood and oil; and that these liquids were applied in various manners. It remains now to be observed, that all Israel were admitted into the Church of God by divers Baptisms. So Paul tells us " they were " all Baptized into Moses in the cloud and in " the sea." The cloud is called a pillar of fire; consequently fire and water, the one above, the other on every side, were both employed in this service. Still, howbeit, there was something wanting to perfect the initiatory service. Before they could enter the tabernacle, or perform any part of its worship, they must be sprinkled with the blood of a sacrifice. Accordingly we are told, that on the day, in which God avouched them to be his people and they avouched him to be their God, "Moses took the blood, "and sprinkled it on the people, and said, be- "hold the blood of the Covenant which God "hath made with you concerning all these words." Exod. xxiv. 8. thus were they all Baptized or initiated into the Covenant of God by cloud and by fire, the symbols of the holy spirit; by the blood of an atoning sacrifice, and by a water, which represented the sufferings of him, from "whose pierced side came forth blood and water."

With respect to the children of the Israelites, they were all admitted into the Church, much in the same manner, in all the after-periods of their state. In the 16th Chapter of Ezekiel, God expresses his treatment of Israel, in the day of his entering into Covenant with them, in terms borrowed from the usages commonly practised on a new born infant. "I washed thee with water, and I anointed thee with oil," ver. 9. This certainly refers to the common modes of washing and anointing their children immediately

ately after the birth. The blood of the circumcision, too, was holy blood, being the figure of the blood of that holy seed, who was then in, and was in due time about to issue by descent from Abraham. In this blood every male-child was sprinkled on the eight day after his birth. It may be added, that as the passover was the first feast appointed by the law, it would appear from the instance of our Saviour, (Luke, 3.) that this was the first festival, to which the Jewish children were admitted. In this case they were introduced to the temple-worship by the sprinkling of blood, as this was an essential part of the service of the passover. Let us now proceed to consider.

## SECT. V.

### *The* BAPTISM *of* JOHN.

John preached in the wilderness that the kingdom of heaven was at hand, or that the Messiah was just about to appear, and that in testimony of faith in this doctrine, every man should submit to be baptized. He tells us at the same time what his baptism is—" I baptise
" you

"you with water." He used no other fluid in this service but water only.

With respect to the manner in which he applied the water nothing is certain. It is evident, indeed, that he baptized in Jordan and Enon, and that Jesus, when baptized of John, had been in the water, as we are told that when he was baptized "he went straightway up out "of the water;" Matt. iii. 6. But whether he was dipped into, or washed in the water, or had it poured on his head, is no where said. To aver any thing positively on this head, is *to add to the scriptures.* We only say that as Jesus was now about to enter on his public service as a prophet and priest, it is most probable that he was not dipped, but washed or rinsed in the same manner as the priest of the law was washed by Moses at the door of the tabernacle, just before he began to perform the business of his sacred function. As the prophet and priest, also, were anointed with the holy oil on the same occasion, so Jesus, soon as he had been washed with water, was anointed with the Holy Spirit. Matt. iii. 16. "He saw the heavens opened unto him, and the Spirit of God de-
"scending

"scending in a dove-like manner, and lighting
"upon him."

The Baptism of John had one end in common with all others; it was a sign of repentance, or of putting on a new character, tincture or dye. It was particularly intended to express faith in his doctrine, That the kingdom of heaven was at hand.

It differed from the Mosaic baptisms, in that it was by water only; in which respect it was also different from the Baptism of Christ. So he says himself; Matt. iii. 11. "I indeed bap-
"tize you with water: but he that cometh af-
"ter me shall baptize you with the Holy Ghost,
"and with fire." Repentance produces water or tears: here a baptism with water only was the most proper sign of repentance; or the most proper fluid to be employed by one who baptized unto repentance. The fire, which enlivens, warms and comforts the heart, was most properly reserved for him, whose doctrine is calculated to fill us with all joy and peace in believing.

Moreover, John's Baptism was only a sign of faith in the Messiah as about to come in a short time: whereas the Baptism of Christ, was intended

tended as an expression of faith in his being already come, or that the kingdom of heaven was begun. Nor does it appear that John baptized in the name of the Father, Son, and Holy Ghost, as was practised in the Christian Baptism.

While John was employed in baptizing, we are told that Jesus also baptized, at least by the ministration of his disciples. Here a question may arise—Whether was this the same Baptism with that which he afterwards established, before he ascended? To this I answer, That it appears evident that it was not the same, but a Baptism of the same kind with that of John—a baptism with water only, in token of the faith of the baptized in the near approach of the kingdom of heaven. For it is clear, that he did not baptize with the Holy Ghost and with fire, till he had ascended to heaven.

We shall only add, That the Baptism of John was of divine authority: it was enjoined him from heaven. John, i. 33. " He that sent me " to baptize with water, the same said unto " me, &c." Keeping this in view we may easily get at the true meaning of what our Lord said to John, when he refused to baptize him, Matt. iii.

iii. 15. "Suffer it to be so now: for thus it becometh us to fulfil all righteousness." Here it is very natural to enquire, what is that righteousness intended in this passage? The righteousness, which it behoved Christ to fulfil was, according to our commentators, the righteousness of the law; but as the Baptism of John was not an institution of the law of Moses, the question is, How could submission to John's Baptism be any part of the righteousness of that law? How could an act fulfil a law, which was not enjoined in that law? This difficulty can only be solved by observing, That although this Baptism was not appointed in the law of Moses, yet it was now a divine appointment. God sent John to baptize all who professed faith in his doctrine. Consequently our Lord could not have obeyed every divine law then in force, if he had not submitted to the Baptism of John. It behoved our Saviour to obey every law of God, whether it was delivered by Moses or afterwards. Therefore, says he to John "suf- "fer it now," for thus I must fulfil not only the law of Moses, or any previous law, but this also which heaven has now appointed.

In this sense John might understand our
Lord's

Lord's words; but he seems to have had something besides in his eye, which would not so readily occur to John. It is evident, that the priest of the law could not enter on the execution of his office, until he was washed with water at the door of the tabernacle of the congregation. Jesus, the high-priest of our profession, was now about to enter on the discharge of his sacred function: and it certainly became him to enter upon his office, according to the law. Though he was not of the order of Aaron, yet the law prophesied of his priesthood, and that he would magnify the law and make it honourable. It was proper, then, that he should be washed with water, in a religious manner, before he entered on the business of the priesthood, That this type in the law might be fulfilled in him. Thus his submission to Baptism was an evidence of his intention to fulfil every part of righteousness.—We now proceed to consider.

## SECT. VI.

### *The* CHRISTIAN BAPTISM.

This Baptism was instituted by Jesus, when all

all power had been given him in heaven and in earth. Juſt before he aſcended he ſaid to his diſciples, "Go, teach all nations, baptizing "them in the name of the Father, Son and "Holy Ghoſt, teaching them to obſerve all "things, whatſoever I have commanded you." This inſtitution was intended to continue in the church of Jeſus, and was not to ceaſe with the life of the apoſtles; for he adds, "Lo, I "am with you all the days until the end, fi- "niſhing or concluſion of the age," *i. e.* the goſpel diſpenſation, or what the Jews called, *the age of the Meſſiah*. Nor is there the leaſt hint, in all the apoſtolic writings, of an intention to relinquiſh the practice of this ſacred rite. We propoſe to offer our thoughts on this ſubject in the following order; 1ſt, we ſhall view the materials uſed in the chriſtian baptiſm; 2d, the mode of their application; and 3dly, the ſubjects of this inſtitution. As to

*The Materials uſed in this Baptiſm.*

We are told, that to the water of John, Jeſus added the Holy Ghoſt and fire. This was foretold by John Baptiſt; Matt. iii. 11. "I "baptize you with water unto repentance: but
"he

"he that cometh after me, he shall baptize you with the Holy Ghost and with fire." This was fulfilled, when the spirit descended in the symbol of fire, first on the Jewish believers on the day of pentecost, Acts ii. 1, 2, 3, 4. and then on the Gentile converts, Acts x. 44, 48. That this was the accomplishment, of the baptists prediction is clear from the use made of it by Peter, Acts xi. 15, 16. " As I began to " speak, the Holy Ghost fell on them, as on us " at the beginning. Then remembered I the " word of the Lord, how that he said, John " indeed baptized with water, but ye shall be " baptized with the Holy Ghost." Our Lord himself promised this kind of baptism just before he ascended. Acts i. 5.

As this baptism of the Holy Spirit or fire was the only baptism promised by Christ to his disciples, the Quakers have hence inferred that water-baptism is not any part of the baptism of Christ. In this, however, they are obviously mistaken. The apostles of Christ undoubtedly understood the meaning of their master's command, when he said " Go and baptize:" and that they always baptized with water, is as evident, as any fact recorded in scripture. To
spend

spend time in proving this point would argue consummate folly.

But, still, it may be asked, Why then does John, and even our Lord himself, only mention the baptism of the Holy Ghost and fire as the christian baptism, if water be also a part of it? The answer is—Nothing else distinguished the baptism of Christ from all others. Water, blood and oil had been employed in the baptisms of the law: John had used water for the same purpose. None of these, then, would have distinguished the baptism of Christ from others. Hence it was called the baptism of the Holy Ghost and fire, because this was its distinguishing characteristic: but this did not say that nothing else was to be used in that service. In like manner, the Lord's supper is called the breaking of bread, although wine also is an essential part of it.

Moreover the pouring out of the Holy Ghost and fire is most properly called the baptism of Christ, because this is his peculiar prerogative. Men may baptize with water; but Jesus alone can baptize with the Holy Ghost. The Apostles must tarry at Jerusalem, until *he* sent upon them the promise of the Father, enduing them with power from on high. The apostles baptized with water on the day of pentecost, Acts ii. but it was Jesus that baptized them with the Holy Ghost. Cornelius and his friends were the first converts to christianity from among the Gentiles. These Peter baptized with water, Acts xx. but it was Jesus that poured on them the Holy Spirit.

I may add, The Quakers would have argued with more plausibility, had they averred that the baptism of the spirit was intended to cease, rather than that of water. The baptism of the spirit was at first visible. It was accompanied with fire, the visible sign of the reality of this baptism. This visible fire soon failed; at least we seldom read of it: whereas we find water constantly employed in every instance of christian baptism we have on record.

Thus we have seen water and fire connected together in the christian baptism. Let us first attend to the divine purpose in continuing, in the Christian church, the use of

*Water-Baptism.*

There has been a religious application of water to the bodies of believers from the beginning

ning, as we have already seen. This was intended to point out the purifying influences of the spirit, or the washing of regeneration, the renewing of the Holy Ghost, purifying us from all iniquity. This is still its design under christianity. Hence, says Peter, Acts ii. 38. "Be baptized every one of you in the name of Jesus Christ, *for the remission of sins.*" To the same purpose says Ananias to Saul, Acts xxii. 16. "Arise, and be baptized, and *wash away thy sins.*"—It seems also to have been intended as a sign of contrition, repentance or sorrow for sin, since John Baptist says, "I baptize with water unto repentance," or as a sign of repentance. The design of John's preaching was to convince men of sin, and to point to the coming saviour. Conviction of sin begets tears, the water of repentance. In this view, with what propriety was John confined to the use of water *only* in his baptism!—The spirit, also, is now come to "convince the world of sin," as well as to wash it away; and consequently we may see some propriety in continuing the the water, as symbolical of these influences, in the religious institutions of the gospel.

But, say the Quakers, visible signs are carnal ordinances and shadows of spiritual things, the body of which is Christ and his church. Christ, the body, is come, for what end then serves the figure? The gospel-church is the true spiritual spouse of Christ, of which the law-church was the figure. What business, then, has a spiritual church with carnal ordinances, purifying the flesh? In this respect, wherein does she differ from the law-church? Particularly, since water used religiously was a figure of the spirit, why should we continue the figure, now the spirit himself is come?— It is impossible to give any satisfactory reply to these objections without attending carefully to the nature and constitution of

## *The Christian Church.*

The word *church* signifies an assembly, congregation or society met together in one place. Thus Israel are called a congregation or church, because they met together in one place, even Jerusalem, to observe the ordinances of worship. For the same reason, the saints in corinth are called a church—they came together into one place to eat the Lord's Supper with its attendant services.—The word church also

means

means all real believers in Christ, whether in heaven or in earth in person; as they are but one congregation, offering up all their services of worship before the one, true altar in the heavenly sanctuary.

By the church of Christ, then, two societies are meant one visible on earth; the other unseen as yet by mortal eyes, although about to be made visible in due time. The one is made up of such as profess the faith of Christ; the other of real believers only. The church on earth has a carnal, earthy as well as a spiritual part, every member having an outward as well as an inward man; whereas that assembly enrolled in heaven is wholly spiritual. Even such of her members as are on earth are only so with respect to the hidden man of the heart." They are in heaven only in spirit, by faith, love, hope and joy. The body cannot enter there till it be made a spiritual body.— hypocrites, too, are in the visible society or church of Christ; but nothing that makes a lie can enter the heavenly sanctuary.

Of these Churches the one is appointed by their Lord as the figure of the other. The church assembling in heaven is the one only true

true church of God, whereof the church below is but a figure or representation. All the members of a visible church on earth profess the faith of Christ, but it is not true that they all have believed in truth. They all "are of Is-"rael, but they are not all Israel." Such a church is indeed true in some respects—she is truly instituted by Jesus Christ—she professes the true faith, observes the true ordinances of worship and discipline appointed by the true head, and has in her a number of the true members of that head. Thus she is the true church in opposition to the false church, which is not instituted by the true head, but is founded on the authority of the kings of this world, holds the faith as modelled and authorized by civil and ecclesiastic authority, and walks after the traditions and commandments of men. Such a church is a false church, indeed, as she lies when she calls herself a church of Christ. To such a church a visible church of Christ is opposed, as with respect to such a church she is true: but with respect to the heavenly church she is a figure. In her church-capacity all her members are not true, yet she is a *true*, *i. e.* a just figure or representation of the true church as her *profession* is the same with that of the church in heaven.

The church visible is instituted for the sake of the invisible. In the church below we have a lively representation of the church above in all her services. In her, also, the members of the invisible or true church are trained up for the services of heaven; in her they are born again, are nourished up in the words of faith and good doctrine, imbibe the sentiments and learn the manners of their father's house. A church on earth, then, is a school of discipline for the son's of God, where they grow up to perfection in the unity of the faith and knowledge of the Son of God.—Thus the visible church not only prefigures or is the image of the invisible, but she trains up her children for her, giving them "to suck at the breasts of her consolations," while they "are delighted with the abundance of her glory".—For so important purpose is a church on earth instituted!

It is easy now to obviate the objection of the Quakers against the use of figures and visible signs in the new testament church. Their objection is founded on a mistake. They imagine that Christ has no church now but the spiritual

or

or heavenly one; whereas it is evident that he has appointed visible churches, which are figures of the true, in the same sense in which the old testament church or congregation was. If the one assembles in one place to worship God according to his institutions, so did the other. If the one be visible, so was the other. The one had hypocrites in her, and so has the other. While the present system stands, there will be something "that offends and does iniquity in the kingdom of christ—tares hid among the wheat. Members of the invisible church have been trained up in both. Thus both have subserved the same purposes. Since, then, a visible church of Christ is still a figure, where lyes the absurdity or even impropriety of appointing figurative ordinances in a figurative church? A visible church must have visible ordinances, or she deserves not the name. So wise, so proper is the conduct of Jesus, in appointing such ordinances in the new testament church! As she has got larger views of the wisdom and love of God, and the spirit of Jesus given her, she is a nobler figure of the church in heaven than the church of old was; so that with respect to her she is called " the kingdom
" of

" of heaven". Yet with respect to the true, the church yet to be revealed, she is earthy, and hence has visible institutions in her still. Though arrived at a higher degree of perfection, still she must have something earthy suited to her state, and to be a figure of good things yet to come.

Keeping this in view, we can easily see the propriety of retaining water-baptism in the christian church. Christ has always come, or has been exhibited in the church of God from the time of the entrance of sin, by water as well as by blood: and since symbols are still necessary in the house of God, none can be imagined more proper than water. Sinners are still called to repentance; and Jesus is exalted a prince and saviour to give repentance and remission of sins, or to cleanse from all unrighteousness. Surely then nothing can more properly express one's faith in this, than by submitting to be baptized in the name of the Lord Jesus.—Jesus still, then, baptizes with water, but to this he has added

*The Baptism of the Holy Ghost and fire.*

The baptism of the Holy Ghost and that of fire are the same. Fire was the external sign or symbol of the presence of the divine spirit. So it was of old. The pillar of cloud and fire was the symbol of the divine presence among Israel, the church of old. Wind and fire are the same to the new testament church. This baptism or initiation was " the promise of the father," of which Christ said he would send it upon his disciples. This is a baptism peculiar to the new testament dispensation, by which the baptism of Christ is distinguished from all other baptisms—" He shall baptise with the " Holy Ghost and fire." Wisdom must appear in this part of the divine plan, as in every other: let us search for her design, that we may see the propriety of adding fire to water in the christian baptism.

1st, Truth in the inward parts constitutes a christian.—Faith working by love is all in Christ Jesus. Water is applied only to the outward parts for the purpose of cleansing; whereas fire penetrates the inward parts of the subject to which it is applied, purging away its dross and
refining

refining it from impurities. In this view, how elegantly was this made the characteristic part of the baptism of Christ! Intimating that Christ is as a refiner's fire, purifying the heart by faith; and that all the true members of the church of Christ must be purified by the sacred fire of heaven, the love of God shed abroad in the heart. Had his religion consisted in externals only, water alone would have been a proper sign; as water cleanses the external parts. But an inward purifier can only be the proper sign of initiation to an inward religion. Both parts of Christ's baptism are prophecied of by Isaiah, "when the Lord shall have washed away the "filth of the daughter of Zion," alluding to water baptism, washing outwardly; as the baptism of the spirit is described in the following words " and shall have purged the blood of Jeru- " salem from *the midst* of her, by the spirit of " judgment and by the *spirit of burning.*" Is. iv. 4. The spirit of fire can only purify the internal part. 2dly, The law, in the Jewish sense of it, or considered in its letter as distinct from the gospel, consisted in carnal services or what Paul calls dead works. The letter kills, and all obedience paid to it was but dead works, or an unanimated service, influenced by the cold, the chilling "spirit of fear." John, too, preached the doctrine of repentance, terrifying men into obedience. This doctrine chilled the heart with fear, and wet the cheek with tears. Water, alone, then, might serve for an initiation into that faith. A cold baptism suited a spirit of fear. But now "God hath not given us the spirit of bondage to fear, " but the spirit of love. He requires no dead works, but living works must serve the living God. Now fire is the vital principle of the universe, the source of motion, the spring of life. How properly, then, did Jesus baptize with fire! He came to give us life: his spirit quickens: his words are spirit and they are life. What could represent this so properly as fire? water may still be a part of the gospel-baptism, as repentance is still a fruit of the gospel; but its water must be animated by fire, since its repentance is not a sorrow to death, but a " repentance unto life." The symbol of life must express a repentance unto life. The very tears of the gospel must be tears of love. The tears of Moses and John were the ofspring of fear; but Jesus loved and wept. He loved Lazarus, and wept

for

for his death: he loved Jerusalem, and wept over her ruins. Love alone sheds the warm, the generous tear. We must look on Jesus ere we can mourn according to the gospel.

3dly, It was proper that fire should be employed on this occasion, to shew that the christian baptism is wholly in the hand of Jesus Christ. The baptism of the spirit can be conferred by no man. It belongs solely to him, who has the spirit without measure in him. To apply water to the body is in every man's power: John could baptize with water. But to purify the spirit of man within him is the province of Jesus Christ. To indicate this truth the sign of fire was highly proper. The fire of heaven is not at the command of man. It is God that answers by fire. Thus the sign and the thing signified corresponded. The sacred fire was always the symbol of Jehovah's presence: it was " the glory of the only-begotten " of the father." The baptism of the spirit then, whereof it was the sign, must be from heaven and not of man.—Here another question must arise to the inquiring mind,

Whether are the baptisms of water and of
the

the Holy Ghoſt always connected under the chriſtian diſpenſation?

I anſwer, not always.—How then, it will be ſaid, can the baptiſm of water be called the chriſtian baptiſm, when not accompanied with the Holy Spirit, ſince the ſpirit is the characteriſtical part of the baptiſm of Chriſt? To find a proper anſwer to this queſtion we muſt look back to what has been ſaid concerning the two ſtates of the chriſtian church, the one viſible and the other inviſible. Now in the firſt or viſible ſtate of the church we are aſſured there will be many hypocrites or falſe profeſſors; the tares will grow with the wheat, till Jeſus come again to gather out of his kingdom all things that offend and all that do iniquity. As a church of this kind has ſomething earthy in her, and all her members have not the ſpirit of Chriſt in them in truth but only in appearance, a baptiſm of water can only be abſolutely neceſſary as a ſign of initiation into the fellowſhip of that church. This baptiſm, therefore, Chriſt has put into the power of the members of that church that they may adminiſter it to as many as profeſs his faith, whether in truth or in hypocriſy. Hence this baptiſm, like every thing elſe

ſtanding

standing in the outer court of the house of God has been, and must be trodden under foot of the Gentiles, or perverted and abused by them until the time of the Gentiles be fulfilled. Nevertheless, this is the baptism of Christ, as he has given it to his visible church, and appointed it to be continued in her until he come to cleanse the sanctuary and make his visible and invisible church the same. He has erected the outer-court as well as the inner: he has his real disciples in the one as well as the other, and the ordinances he has appointed correspond to these respective courts. He has made the one court the entrance to the other. We must not then despise or neglect any of his appointments, knowing that if we be ashamed of him or of his words before men, of us he will be ashamed before his father.

Yet as his true kingdom is within men, his real church is not visible in her present state. Hence he has retained the true baptism in his own hand, that he may administer it to all, whom the father has given him. The invisible baptism is left in the unseen hand, and he will not fail to administer it to all who have a tittle to it, although he has not bound himself to confer it at the very moment of the administration of water-baptism.

Thus both baptisms are Christ's, although that of the Holy Spirit be his in a peculiar sense. They are but one baptism, however, as they both combined make but the one complete baptism of Christ, and initiate one into both courts of his house. The one is visible and the other invisible, suited to the different states of his church in the present dispensation of things.— It will now be asked, since fire was the symbol of the baptism of the Holy Spirit,

Why was the sign of fire discontinued immediately after the commencement of the christian dispensation among Jews and Gentiles?

To this we answer—To ascertain the presence of the Holy Spirit, it was necessary that fire should come down on the apostles and disciples of Christ at first. The world could not have been certain that the Holy Ghost had descended on them, had they not seen the visible symbol of his presence: nor could the disciples have been sure, that their masters had found acceptance with the father, and that he had sat down on his throne, if he had not sent the promised token of his acceptance and exaltation.

When

When about to leave them he said " depart not from Jerusalem, but wait for the promise of the Father, which ye have heard of me. For John truly baptized with water, but ye shall be baptized with the Holy Ghost, not many days hence—The same shall baptize you" said John, " with the Holy Ghost and fire." Had not this fire descended on them, then, it is evident the promise would not have been accomplished, and consequently they would have had no foundation for faith in the exaltation of Jesus to the throne. But this fact being now ascertained by the most unequivocal evidence, there could be no necessity for the continuance of this appearance of fire in the church of Christ. When he promised to send the spirit, he assured his disciples that he should abide with them and should be in them, and that for ever; and that his presence should be known by his fruits: Love is the true fire of which the visible fire was but a symbol. This is an abiding fruit and evidence of the spirit, present with all that believe. " For by one spirit are we all baptized into one body, whether we be Jews or Gentiles." The baptism of the Holy Ghost, then, still remains, and still is in fire, even divine love

love, which has "the flames of God". Now abideth, faith, hope and love".

But it may be said, might not the water also have ceased, after the spirit came, of whom it was but the sign as well as fire? This is the opinion of the Quakers, but founded in a mistake. Water was not only the symbol of the spirits influences, but it was intended as a sign of initiation into a visible society. Now a visible society must have visible institutions, and consequently some visible sign of admission into that society. Hence the propriety of the continuance of water-baptism in the church of Jesus. But fire was intended to be a sign of the actual communication of the Holy Spirit to the church in his gifts of miracles, tongues &c. and these extraordinary influences were not intended to abide, neither was there any necessity that their sign should continue. Again, so far as the fire was the sign of love, it was a sign of admission into the unseen or real church, and an invisible church needs no visible sign of admission into her fellowship.

As all the extraordinary, miraculous gifts of the spirit have now ceased, fire could only be the sign of his abiding fruits, faith, hope and love

love. In this cafe, if fire fhould defcend on all *profeffed* believers, it would be a *falfe* fign: and if it fell only on *real* believers, it would diftinguifh the wheat from the tares even in this world, and make the church vifible and invifible the fame, contrary to the declared intention of providence. Such wifdom appears in the ceafing of the external fign of fire, when the age of miracles ended.

It may be obferved here, that baptifm with water is diftinguifhed from that of the Holy Spirit—" John baptized with water, but ye fhall " be baptized with the Holy Ghoft." There is a high propriety in this diftinction. Water-baptifm is no infallible fign of the prefence of the divine fpirit, nor was ever intended to be fo. Fire only has this honour. External fire was the fign of the prefence of the Holy Spirit in his extraordinary, unabiding gifts; and the internal fire appearing in its native fruits is the fign of his prefence in his faving, abiding gifts of faith, hope and love. Hence our Lord faid, " by *this* fhall all men *know* that ye are my dif-" ples, if ye *love* one another." Water-bapifm is the external fign of introduction into my church,

church, but baptism with the spirit of love is the only infallible sign of real discipleship.

The baptism of the Holy Ghost, then, is the baptism of the church of Christ as invisible, as baptism of water pertains to his church as visible. The latter is in the hand of men to be administred to all who profess the faith of Christ: the former is solely in the hand of Christ, that he may bestow it on such as are really his. These constitute the one, complete baptism of Christ, and his baptism will have these two parts, while his church is viewed in two aspects, visible and unseen. Water-baptism is to be respected as his ordinance, as well as the other; and as a subjection to his appointments is necessarily connected with believing in him, hence our Lord says, " he that believeth, and is baptized, shall " be saved," *q d* he that believeth, and confesseth, the same, by submitting to my institutions, shall be saved.—Let us now proceed to consider

## SECT VII.

*The mode of this Baptism.*

Looking into the old testament, we have
found

found a variety of modes practised by the church of the living God, in the application of fluids to the body for a religious purpose: and that all these are called baptism is evident from what Paul says, Heb: ix. 10. The law consisted of "diverse baptisms." We have seen them diverse in the *means* used for purification, viz, water, blood and oil; as also in the *mode* of application, viz, by *washing* or *rinsing*, *anointing* or *pouring upon, bathing, putting upon, sprinkling*. So properly are they called "diverse baptisms."

Let us now see whether or not our Lord specified any of these well known modes, as essentially necessary to be observed in the christian baptism. For this end let us read the words of institution—"Go ye and teach all nations, bap-" tizing them in the name of the Father, and " of the Son, and of the Holy Ghost; teach-" ing them to observe all things, whatsoever " I have commanded you." Now as our Lord knew very well that diverse modes of baptism had been used by divine appointment in the old testament church, if he had meant to make any particular mode essentially necessary to his baptism, he would have certainly specified it on this occasion, to prevent mistakes. Yet this he nowhere

nowhere does—a plain evidence that he did not see it necessary. The nature and import of of baptism was perfectly well known to the apostles, as well as all the modes of performing it. If dipping them, had been meant by him as the only mode of his baptism, how strange is it that this mode should be left unascertained, and to suffer his disciples to run the risk of mismanagement in the discharge of their office! What can be inferred from this circumstance, then, but that Jesus did not intend to make any particular mode of the application of water essential to his baptism? In this case, his apostles needed no particular description of baptism, as it is so clearly marked, in all its various modes, in the old testament: and as their master specified no particular mode, they would naturally conclude that they were left at full liberty in this respect.

2dly. Let us now see in what sense the apostles actually understood our saviour's words, when he commanded them to baptize. This we must learn from their words and practice: and if on examining these, we find that they considered *dipping* as synonimous with baptizing,

this

this must determine the point, as they certainly underſtood their commiſſion.

Here the baptiſts only fix upon one inſtance, which they reckon ſufficient to determine the apoſtolic mode of baptizing, viz. that recorded in Acts viii. 38. There we are told Philip and the Eunuch " went down both *into* the water" where Philip baptized the Eunuch; and when this was performed, we have them coming " *out* of the water." A weak argument, indeed, in favour of dipping! the whole ſtreſs of it lies on the Greek word εις, rendered *into;* and if this ſignifies plunging, then Phillip and the Eunuch muſt have been both plunged on this occaſion, as it is equally applied to both—" They " went down both into the water." Had it been ſaid, that Phillip put the Eunuch *into* the water, this would have concluded in favours of dipping; but as the words ſtand, they conclude nothing, only that they both went down at leaſt to the brink of the water. For, it muſt be obſerved, that the Greek εις moſt properly ſignifies *unto*. This, then, does not ſay that they entered into the water; or even ſuppoſing that they went a ſhort way into it, it does not neceſſarily follow from thence that either of

E                                              them

them were plunged: and as to their coming "*out* of the water," if a man goes down to drink or to wash his feet in a water, when he returns, we can most properly say he came up out of the water.

With respect to the argument taken from John's baptism, it is equally inclusive. True, Jesus was baptized of John in Jordan, but whether by immersion or anointing is no where said. The word *us* will not warrant any determinate conclusion. But supposing that he used immersion, can we aver that he was restricted to that mode; or even allowing that he was, can we merely from this circumstance conclude any thing positively concerning the mode of christian baptism? The question is not How John baptized; but whether Christ has appointed any particular mode of baptism?

We have many instances of the apostles baptizing recorded in their history, but from none of them can we ascertain the manner of their administration. It is most probable, however, that immersion was not used by them, at least in many instances. Three thousand were baptized on the day of the Spirit's descent; but it is not said that they went out of the city to the

brook

*A Dissertation on Baptism.*

brook Kidron to be plunged. It is more probable that they were baptized in the temple, by anointing, washing, or sprinkling with water. Nor is it probable that the Jaylor and his houshold were taken to a river to be baptized at the hour of mid-night. This would have been highly dangerous. It seems probable, that this ordinance was performed in the prison, as we find water there, wherewith the Jaylor washed the stripes of the prisoners. As in the same verse we are told he " washed their " stripes, and was baptized, he and all his, " straightway," it is almost certain, that a part of the same water was employed in his baptism, that he had used in washing the stripes of Paul and Silas. Acts xvi. 25—33.

3dly, The effusion of the Holy Ghost on the disciples is expressly called the baptism of Christ, and more properly so than that of water. Now in what manner were they baptized with the Holy Ghost? Of this we have a full instance recorded in Acts x. 44, 45—" On the " Gentiles also was *poured out* the gift of the Holy " Ghost." This Peter expressly calls baptism, in giving an account of that great event, Acts xi. 16. " Then remembered I the word of the " Lord,

"Lord, how that he said, John indeed baptized with water; but ye shall be baptized with the Holy Ghost." Now if this *pouring upon* was not one of the modes of Baptism, how, does Christ and his apostle uniformly call it by that name? Yea, as water-baptism was but a sign of this true baptism of Christ, we may certainly conclude that there must be a strong analogy between the sign and the thing signified; and that in the history of the *true baptism* we must find the *true mode* of baptism.

Mr M'Lean seems to be galled with this argument, and hence he employs a great deal of pains to evade it, but with no success. Baptism in the Holy Ghost is expressed by *pouring him out* on men, *anointing, the washing of regeneration, sprinkling,* but he says, "none of them "so much as allude to baptism." He owns, indeed, that "the extraordinary effusion of the "spirit is called baptism, but not in strict propri- "ety of speech, but in allusion to baptism in wa- "ter." A very odd assertion, indeed! John baptist and our Lord Jesus Christ uniformly, and the apostles frequently, call this effusion baptism; but it seems they did not know how to speak properly, but called an action baptism, while there

there is not the most distant similitude between the one and the other. Whereas any person, unbyassed by party, must see that this is the most plain and expressive term that could have been chosen for this purpose. Men, at least since the time of Moses, had been always initiated into the church of God and her offices, by anointing or pouring on them, washing, sprinkling, &c. all of which were called Baptism or initiation, as we have seen already. How, then, could our Lord have chosen a more proper word, or one more intelligible, when he would express the action of giving the Holy Spirit? But a favourite tenet must be supported at any expence. The effusion of the spirit is baptism says Jesus: No, says Mr M'Lean; there is not the least resemblance between the one and the other. Instead of allowing Jesus to speak properly, he will not allow him to speak even metaphorically; since every metaphor is a simile, or founded on similitude.

On this plan, we may as well argue that water-baptism is not properly so called, but merely in allusion to the baptism of the spirit. This assertion would have a more plausible appearance

ance; since water baptism was intended to represent the baptism of the spirit.

4thly, In the apostolic allusions to baptism, when they refer to the *action* itself, we find them always expressing it by *washing, pouring upon, anointing, or sprinkling*. Thus in Titus iii. 5. 6. the baptism of the spirit is called " the " washing of regeneration, the renewing of the " Holy Ghost; which he shed or poured on us " abundantly, through Jesus Christ our Savi-" our." Again, in Heb. x. 22. the apostle speaks of both the baptisms of Christ, and uses *sprinkling* and *washing* indifferently in expressing their application, the one to the body, the other to the heart—" Let us draw near with a " true heart, in the full assurance of faith, ha-" ving our hearts sprinkled from an evil con-" science, and our bodies washed with pure " water." All these several modes of the religious application of a fluid to a man are called " baptisms" by Paul, Heb. ix. 10. consequently all of them may be properly called baptism, and are so called accordingly, as is evident from the above instances. Dipping only, then, is not the mode of christian baptism.

5thly, This view is farther confirmed from what

what our Lord himself says, John xiii. 8, 9, 10. When washing his disciples' feet, he takes occasion to introduce a hint of a more important washing, which he would perform on all his people—" If I wash thee not, thou hast no part " in me." The washing here mentioned is such a one as gives a part with Christ or in Christ. Now, it is evident, that there are two washings which give a man a part with Christ; the washing with water applied to the body in baptism, and the washing of regeneration by the renewing of the Holy Spirit. By the former one obtains a part in the visible state of the church of Christ, and without this washing no man can be admitted to her fellowship. By the latter we are admitted to a spiritual communion with Christ, or to be members of his church invisible, vitally united to him. Baptism then must be the washing he here intends, since thereby we obtain a part in him, and by no other washing at all. The complete baptism of Christ sprinkles the heart from an evil conscience by faith in the resurrection of Christ from the dead, and washes the body with pure water. " He that believes and is baptized shall be saved" or have a part in Christ.—But must the

the whole body be plunged in water, when Christ thus washes us? So Peter imagined "Lord, not my feet only but also my hands "and my head." But what says his master? —"He that is washed, needeth not, save to "wash his feet, but is clean every whit." Here, I think it evident, he cannot be speaking of any common washing of an unclean body, since in this case, washing the feet could not possibly cleanse the whole body from pollution. It remains then to conclude, that he is speaking of baptism, and as if he had foreseen the mighty stress that would be laid upon dipping the whole body in water, in future periods of his church, he gives them the strongest caveat against such a notion, by telling them that washing a part makes the whole clean.

In this view the baptism of water corresponds to the baptism of the spirit. The christian is only renewed in the spirit of his mind. Whatever influence this new spirit, created in him may have upon his body, yet his body is not made new. The body is still dead because of sin, and has fleshly lusts warring in its members. The inner man, then, is clean, while the outward man has sin dwelling in him. Yet the

renovation

renovation of the mind secures the renovation of the body, when it shall be changed and fashioned like Christ's most glorious body. Then he will quicken our mortal bodies, by the spirit, which he has given us. Supposing then a a part of the body only washed in baptism, water-baptism will the more exactly answer to the baptism of the spirit, in which only a part of the man is washed.

This view will also teach us the propriety of our Lord's saying, when a part is washed the whole is clean. The purification of the mind by the spirit of believing secures to us the purification of the whole man in due time. Thus the whole may be said to be clean. The God of peace will sanctify us wholly in soul, body and spirit.

6thly, We have seen that the Jewish priest was sprinkled with blood, when initiated to his office; which sprinkling is called baptism by our Lord; when with reference to that action he says " I have a baptism to be baptized with, " and how am I straitened till it be accomplish-" ed." Ere I can enter the most Holy place, I must be baptized with the blood of my sacrifice. Sure this was not performed by dipping.

The

The above arguments seem to me conclusive We have examined the words in which Christ instituted his baptism; the practice of his Apostles in performing that service, and the words in which they describe it. In short, we have taken a survey of all the baptisms mentioned in sacred writ, and yet cannot find plunging any where mentioned as the alone baptism of Christ—Let us now see what Mr M'Lean says in support of his favourite dogma.

He avers " that any other sign than *immersi-*" *on,* be what it will, is not Christ's ordinance, " either in name or thing, and therefore can " in no respect be a proper representation, but " a human invention, whereby the law of Christ " is made void." A bold assertion indeed: But how is it supported? Why,

1st, By an elaborate criticism on a Greek word. βαπτιζω signifies to *dip, immerse* or *plunge*—Pity it is, ye illiterate christians, that ye are not adepts in the Greek tongue: Without this you cannot, it seems, know the law of Christ, who has made the faith of his disciples hang on a critical knowledge of a Greek word. Now since so much stress is laid on this criticism, let us see how far it will go to support the cause.

2dly,

2dly, The Greek word βαπτω is the root of βαπτιζω and it signifies *dyeing, staining, colouring;* and as this is generally performed by immersion, hence the same word means *washing, dipping,* as is evident from the Lexicons. If we must adhere then to the strict sense of the word, we must *dye* or add a *new colour* to the person baptized. In this very sense, it is literally applied to a certain order of priests, of whom we read in *Aristophanes,* who were called βαπτοι not from being immersed, but from their staining their bodies with a certain colour, as a badge of distinction. Hence the Latins called them *fucati.* We may as well argue, then, that there is no man baptized who is not dyed, as that there is none baptized, that is not immersed.

The truth is, the initiating ordinance of christianity seems to be called baptism, because we then take on a new tincture or colour, *i. e.* a new character. To be " baptized into Christ" and to " put on Christ" are synonimous expressions: and to put on Christ is to put on his character. How easily, then, could an ingenious critic argue in favours of dyeing the body as a sign of the soul putting on a new character!

3dly,

3dly, It is admitted that this word means *dipping* or *immersion;* yet this will not conclude in favour of Mr M'Lean. Every ordinance must have a name; and as immersion is the full and perfect application of a fluid to the body, it was most natural to call this ordinance *baptism*, since it consists in applying water to the body. But how absurd is it to argue from hence, that there is no baptism but by immersion, contrary to the whole tenor of scripture. The question is not whether immersion be baptism; but whither this be the only sense of the word? We must permit the apostles to explain their own meaning; and I trust it is evident from what has been said, that their sense of this word extends to every religious application of water to the body, in whatever mode it be applied.

4thly, The christian ordinance of bread and wine is called by the apostles *the Lord's Supper*. If, then, in observing this institution, we must adhere to the strict literal sense of the terms, it can only be observed at the ordinary time of supper. According to Mr M'Lean's plan of reasoning, we must aver " that any other method of eating it, whether in the morning or at noon, " is not Christ's ordinance, either in
" name

"name or thing, but a human invention, where-
"by the law of Chrift is made void." Neither breakfaft nor dinner is fupper; but Chrift appointed a fupper; Therefore to eat at any other time is not to eat the Lord's fupper.—So fome have argued: and their argument is precifely of the fame kind with this gentleman's.

I may add, that the word rendered *dip* does not neceffarily fignify a *total* immerfion. Thus Lev. iv. 6. "The prieft fhall *dip* his finger "in the blood, and fprinkle of the blood." Now every body knows that dipping the finger does not neceffarily mean dipping the whole finger, but a part of it. One is faid to dip his finger in a liquid, when the point of it only is dipped. Thus even where bapt-ei evidently means dipping it does not include total immerfion. Yet this is a principal text, produced by Mr M'Lean in fupport of his argument; from which he fays very ftrong words againft fuch as fprinkle or pour inftead of plunging: They are "guilty, he fays, of rebellion againft "the Lord and may juftly expect immediate "vengeance." Strong words, but weak arguing! Little did this zealous man fee that this text is ftrong in favour of his opponents. Here is a real baptism. The priest (bapsei) dipped his finger in the blood, and then sprinkled it as God appointed. This is the precise plan of our baptism. We dip our fingers in the water and sprinkle it on the candidate for baptism. Thus no baptism is performed still but dipping is the first act of it.

How weak is the following observation! " Had the priest presumed to convert *bapto* " here into *sprinkling* or *pouring*, he would " have perverted the whole of this typical in- " stitution." A very idle supposition indeed ! It supposes an impossibile case. How could the priest sprinkle the blood with his finger before he dipped it in the blood. 2. The *second* argument Mr M'Lean produces in support of plunging is as follows—"Nither *sprinkling* nor *pouring* will make sense, when substituted in place " of the word baptize." The very reverse is the truth. Some texts will not read, when the word *plunged* is substituted for baptize. Thus for instance, " plunged into Moses," 1. Cor. x. 2. " plunged into Christ," Rom. vi. 3. This supposes Moses and Christ to be liquids. Again, " Into what were ye plunged" Acts xix. 3. By this reading the question seems to be
—In

—In what water were ye plunged; whereas Paul meant to ask—Into what faith were ye baptized? Also "I indeed *plunge* you in water"—he shall *plunge* you in the Holy Ghost." Now, did Christ really plunge them in the Holy Ghost? Are we not expressly told that the spirit was *poured* on them? And I should be glad to know, by what rule of interpretation, we must make *baptize* signify *pouring upon* in the one clause of a verse and plunging in the other? To make it read consistently, we must read it thus—"I poured water upon you, but he shall pour upon you the holy Ghost; or rather, There is no reference here to the *mode* of baptism at all, but to the materials of it—I initiated you into my faith by water, but he shall initiate you by the Holy Ghost.

Mr M'Lean is equally unhappy in his attempts at wit in the application of the word *poured*, which he says, 'answers only to liquids, 'not persons.' Every body knows, that the English word *pour* has sometimes *out* and sometimes *upon* affixed to it, as the sense and construction require. When applied to persons, it has *upon* affixed. Let this be done in the passages he quotes, and the impropriety disappears.

Add to this, that *water* is evidently supposed in many passages where the verb *baptize* occurs, whether you render it *plunge pour*, or *sprinkle*. Thus " baptized into Christ" cannot be rendered ' plunged into Christ' without implying *in water*. Let this gentleman only allow the same liberty to others, and all the passages he quotes can be rendered either of the ways mentioned, with equal propriety. Thus " Teach all nations, *pouring water upon them* into the name, &c. And had water poured " upon them by " John in Jordan. He that believeth and has " water poured upon him." The same may be said of the word *sprinkle*. " Sprinkling " them with water into the name, &c.—He must be ignorant of the language indeed, who knows not that many phrases in one language cannot bear a literal translation into another; but must be translated in different terms and phrases, according to the sense of the passage, and the analogy of the language into which it is translated. Had this been attended to, this long string of quibbles on the word *baptize* would never have seen light.

Equally absurd is his criticism on the Greek ῳ and ῳ at the bottom of p. 62. He avers that

that both must be rendered the same way when speaking of baptism; and that because, in this case, εις cannot be rendered *with*, neither can εν be so translated. Yet this same writer renders them differently, the one *in*, the other *into*; and that εις and εν have very different senses, even when baptism is the subject, is clear from the passages he refers to. Is it possible to conceive that εν prefixed to ὕδατι has the same sense with εις prefixed to τον Μωσην or χριστον? The former always signifies *in, with* or *by*; the latter, *into* or *unto* the name, profession or faith of Moses or Christ. Again, when εν is prefixed to πνευματι ἁγιω it cannot be rendered *in*, whatever way the word *baptize* be translated, whether *plunge*, *sprinkle* or *pour upon*. Thus " he shall *plunge*, " *dip, sprinkle* or *pour upon* you in the Holy " Ghost" would be consummate nonsense. Yet " he shall plunge in the Holy Ghost" is the version given us by this critic's rule!—Miserable, absurd, and despicable criticism.

As to his 3d and 4th arguments, taken from the circumstances of our Lord's baptism and that of the Eunuch; together with the places where John baptized, we have already found them inconclusive, and shall therefore proceed

F 3

to confider his 5th, taken from the allufions, which the apoftles make to baptifm.

Paul alludes to, or rather plainly expreffes, the action of baptifm by various phrafes, as *wafhing, fprinkling, pouring upon &c.*; but, this gentleman only finds one phrafe, in which he imagines any fuch allufion appears, viz. "buried "with him by baptifm, wherein alfo ye are ri- "fen with him." Here, he fuppofes, that there muft be a literal burial in baptifm, to give a full fenfe to this phrafe; or that we muft be literally buried under water, as Chrift was under the earth. But here it muft be obferved, that Paul fays alfo, at the very fame time, that we are " baptized into Chrift's death," or " are " planted into the likenefs of his death," Rom. vi. 3, 5. which likenefs of his death he expreffly calls crucifixion, ver. 6. " Knowing this that " our old man is crucified with him." Hence, he fays, " we are dead with Chrift, and cruci- " fied with him;" and that in baptifm. Now, will it not follow hence, that, if to give propriety to the phrafe " buried with him in baptifm," we muft be literally buried, when baptized, to give propriety to the phrafes, " dead with Chrift " and crucified with him," there muft be a literal

teral death and crucifixion in baptism; otherwise it is no proper sign of the thing signified? Thus by equal force of argument, we must conclude, that Mr McLean's baptism "is no in-"stitution of Christ, but a mere human ordi-"nance," since in it there is no literal death, nor any sign of the cross.—The truth is, Paul is not speaking of the mode, but of the great end and design of baptism.'

Finally, the practice of the churches, soon after the apostolic period, has been adduced in support of *dipping;* and it is readily admitted that this mode was commonly practised in these churches. But this argument will go for nothing, when it is considered 1st, That immersion was one of the modes of baptism, and the most perfect application of water to the body; which might give occasion to such critics as Mr McLean to argue that it is the only proper mode. 2dly, Bathing was, and still is, a common practice in these warm climes; which circumstance would naturally induce them to use this mode generally in baptism; from whence bigots might aver that this is the only mode of divine appointment. But that this was not the general opinion of these churches is certain. For, 3dly, although

although they generally used immersion in baptism, yet they considered perfusion or sprinkling as lawful also, as is clear from many of their writings. I shall only quote a passage from *Cyprian's* answer to one *Magnus*, who wrote to him desiring his opinion on this point, he tells him ' that as far as he could conceive, he
' apprehended that the divine benefits could in
' no wise be mutilated, or weakened, not that
' less thereof could be bestowed, where the di-
' vine gifts are received with a sound and full
' faith, &c. For in baptism, the spots of sin
' are washed away otherwise than the filth of
' the body in a secular and carnal bath is, in
' which there is need of a seat to sit upon, of
' a vat to wash in, of soap and other such in-
' gredients, that so the body may be washed
' and cleansed; but in another manner is the
' heart of a believer washed, otherwise is the
' mind of a man purified by the merits of Christ.
' Nor let any one think it strange that the sick
' when they are baptized, are only perfused or
' sprinkled, since the scripture says by the Pro-
' phet Ezekiel, Chap. 36. ver. 25, 26. I will
' sprinkle clean water upon you, and ye shall
' be clean, &c. Also it is said, Numb. xix. 19.
' 20.

'20.—That soul shall be cut off from Israel, because the water of aspersion has not been sprinkled on him. Again, the Lord said to Moses, Numb. viii. 6. 7. Take the Levites and cleanse them—sprinkle water of purifying upon them. And again, the water of aspersion is purification. From whence, it appears that sprinkling is sufficient instead of immersion, and whensoever it is done, if there be a sound faith—it is *perfect* and *complete*.

To this we may add, that the church of Rome, is the first, we read of, that called in question the validity of baptism by perfusion. There the ordination of *Novatian* to be a presbyter was opposed by all the clergy, and by many of the laity, (as *Cornelius* in his epistle to *Fabius* of Antioch tells us,) because he had been baptized by perfusion or sprinkling. So early did the seeds of superstition take root in the Roman church!

Upon the whole, the divine wisdom shines conspicuous in the institution of baptism. Christ's commands are not grievous: his yoke is easy and his burden is light. Christianity was intended to be the religion of all climes and nations, and of men of every state of body, health-ful

ful and fickly, valid and infirm. But if our Lord had made immerfion effential to his baptifm, it is eafy to fee, that his yoke would have been grievous, as there are many climes of the earth and ftates of the human body, in which plunging would be highly dangerous. What wifdom and goodnefs, then, appears in an inftitution, which prefcribes nothing hurtful to the body, while it would fave the foul! There were diverfe modes of baptifm of old. Jefus has left it to his difciples to ufe either of thefe modes, as fhall be found moft convenient. In this cafe, though Mr M'Lean blames our tranflators for leaving the Greek *baptizo* untranflated in our englifh verfion of the new teftament, in this inftance they have acted with judgment. *Wafhing*, indeed, might perhaps have anfwered the purpofe; but no other englifh word could have conveyed the true fenfe of the original.

I fhall only add on this part of the fubject, that notwithftanding the baptifts ftickle fo much concerning the mode of baptifm, no fect whatever deviates fo widely from fcripture and common fenfe in the performance of it. In common life, when one intends to wafh or bathe his body or any thing elfe by immerfing it in water,

he

he puts no covering of any kind upon it. The Jews, Mahometans and Bramins in their religious immersions always perform the ceremony naked. When Moses washed or baptized the priests at the door of the tabernacle, Lev. viii. 7, 8 he put no cloths on them till the sacred rite had been performed. The Russians baptize by immersion to this day; but the baptized are unclothed. Indeed how can a body be washed otherwise? Immersing one with his cloths on may wash the garment but not the man. Will any person act such a part in common life? Or is there a scripture-example for it? In this respect the common mode has propriety in it. It applies water to the face or head, an uncovered part of the body, not the garment. The baptists, properly speaking, wash or baptize the garment and not the man.

Finally, the baptists boast much of the practise of the first churches after the apostles as confirming the argument for immersion. But they certainly know also that these churches used the *triple* immersion, as the Russians do still; or they plunged *first* in the name of the Father; *again*, in the name of the Son; and, *thirdly*, in the name of the Holy Ghost. Is this not as strong an argument for the triple immersion as for immersion itself? Perhaps both may have an equal claim to apostolical authority. Why, then, do we retain the one and abandon the other?

We shall now proceed to consider

## SECT. VIII.

### *The* SUBJECTS *of* BAPTISM.

The baptists confine this institution to believing adults, and triumph over such as practise infant-baptism. For this practice, they tell us, we have neither precept nor example in the new testament, and consequently we are guilty of *will-worship* in observing a human Institution, as a part of religious worship.——These are very heavy charges indeed. We shall examine the justness of them afterwards. In the meantime let us see, whether they may not, with equal force, be retorted upon the accusers themselves.

Supposing, for a moment, that we can neither shew precept nor example in the new testament for infant-baptism, the baptists themselves will be as much at a loss to produce a single

gle inftance of their prefent practice of adult-baptifm from that facred book. That the apoftles were commanded to baptize adult Jews or heathens, on their profeffing the faith of Chrift, and that we have many inftances of this practice in the new teftament, is admitted; but this is nothing to the purpofe. The baptifts not only baptize fuch adults as were never baptized before; but alfo the adult offspring of believers, and fuch as were baptized in their infancy in the name of the Lord Jefus Chrift. For this they have neither precept nor example. Although the facred hiftory of the chriftian church reaches downwards to at leaft thirty years after her firft erection on the day of pentecoft, during which period many infants of believing parents muft have grown up to an adult age, yet we have not one fingle inftance, in all that hiftory, of the adminiftration of baptifm to any adults, fprung of believing parents. If, then, infant-baptifm was not practifed at that time, it muft appear ftrange, that there is no inftance on record of any one born of believers applying for baptifm, when come to adult age. Had we but one example of this kind it would be decifive on this point; and furely

G                 if

if there had been any such a case, we might expect at least to find one such on record. The silence of the scriptures, then, on this point, affords a strong presumption that the children of believers were baptised in infancy, and consequently it furnishes us with a very powerful argument against the present practice of the baptists, who in this respect walk without any example in the footsteps of the flock of Christ. —The same may be said of their re-baptizing such as, in their infancy, have been baptized in the name of the Lord Jesus. No such practice is examplified in any part of sacred writ.

Thus, in these respects, the baptists have no ground to glory over their opponents. Want of scripture-precept or example for their practice is at least as strong against the one as the other.

As to the charge of will-worship in observing a human institution as a religious ordinance, it is without foundation. That baptism is a divine institution is allowed on both sides. To apply this to infants may be a misapplication or abuse of the ordinance of Christ: but this is the worst that can be said of it. To misapply an institution is not to change the nature of it but to mistake its intention. Baptism, then,

is

is still a divine ordinance, although men may abuse it, or through mistake apply it to an improper subject.—I may add, that if the misapplication of an ordinance of Christ can transform it into a mere human institution, as the baptists aver, then they themselves cannot plead innocence. Real believers *only*, according to their scheme, have a right to baptism. Now, can any baptizer among them, in this case, aver that he has never misapplied baptism in any instance? It is indisputable, that they have plunged many, who were yet in the gall of bitterness and bond of iniquity, and consequently, on their own principles, have been guilty of the very crime, so virulently charged against their opponents. If they alledge in their own vindication, that this is done through mistake, and not from any dishonest intention; why do they not make the same allowance for others, who, I dare say, are as honest in applying baptism to infants, as the baptists are in applying that institution to unworthy adults? Both parties may mistake the proper subjects of baptism, in many instances; but neither have any intention of changing the ordinance of Christ into a human institution.

Thus far we have seen both parties on a level. Let us now examine the scriptures, that we may see whether any light, arising from them, leads to the usage of infant-baptism.

In the first place, here, it is necessary that we should consider the commission itself—"Go ye and disciple all nations, baptizing them in the name of the Father," &c. According to these words, the nations are the subjects of baptism, and no nation is excluded. Accordingly the apostles began to execute this commission at Jerusalem, among the Jews first, and afterwards among the Gentiles of all nations. That they baptized adults, professing the faith of Christ, is allowed on all hands: the question is, Whether this commission extends to infants?

In answer to this question, we must observe, That baptism stands in the same place in the new state of the church, that circumcision filled in the old. Both are religious institutions: both intended as solemn initiations into the church of the living God. In this light the apostles understood baptism. So Paul calls it "the circumcision of Christ;" as is clear from Colos. ii. 11, 12. "In whom also ye are cir-
"cumcised

"cumcised—by the circumcision of Christ, buried with him in baptism." The Judaizers in the church of Colosse strenuously maintained the necessity of circumcision in order to obtain salvation. Very well, says Paul; in this respect christians are also complete in Christ. The circumcision mentioned in the law is twofold, one made by hands in the flesh; the other the circumcision of the heart, " made without hands, " in putting off the body of the sins of the " flesh." In the same manner, In Christ we have the circumcision of the heart or spirit, consisting in putting off the body of the sins of the flesh, or in giving up the old man to be crucified with him; and also an external sign of this in the baptism of water applied to the body, Thus in Christ we have a full circumcision. Putting off the old man with his deeds is the thing signified by the circumcision of the flesh; and the same is signified by baptism,

This shews us, by the bye, the absurdity of the Quakers argument from this text against water-baptism. Say they, the circumcision of Christ is expressly said not to be made with hands; consequently his baptism is not of water, as it is applied by the hand.—Now if there

be any force in this argument, it will equally conclude againſt circumciſion in the fleſh as againſt the baptiſm of the fleſh. They themſelves allow, that the carnal circumciſion was a divine appointment under the law. Yet the prophets told the Jews that this availed nothing without the circumciſion of the heart. Deut. xxx. 6. Jer. iv. 4. Paul ſays the ſame thing—" Circum-
" ciſion is that of the heart, in the ſpirit, and
" not of the letter. Neither is that circumci-
" ſion, which is outward in the fleſh." He and Peter alſo ſays the ſame thing of the baptiſm of Chriſt—It is " not made with hands;
" it is not the putting away the filth of the fleſh,
" but the anſwer of a good conſcience." How ſtupid is, it then, to conclude that circumciſion of the fleſh was a divine ordinance, while baptizing the fleſh is not ſo! Do not the ſcriptures ſpeak of both in the ſame ſtyle? The ſenſe is obvious to every man of plain underſtanding—The putting off the old man is the truth or true ſenſe of circumciſion and baptiſm; and conſequently no man is truly baptized or circumciſed, while theſe inſtitutions have only reached his fleſh. The heart is the proper ſubject of both. Yet this does not ſay, that theſe

external

external services were not of divine appointment as figures of the inward effects of the spirit. Although it ever was true, that he is not a Jew who is *only* so outwardly, yet it was also true, that he is not a Jew who is not so outwardly, or who is not circumcised in the flesh.—Sophistry and false reasoning have misled the Quakers as well as others.

2dly, That the apostles understood baptism as a sign of the same nature and import with circumcision, is evident from what has been said. We now add, that hence they found baptism and circumcision on the same promise. Be you circumcised, said God to Abraham, because the covenant or promise is to you and your seed after you, in their generations, for an everlasting covenant Gen. xvii. 7—14. In the same phraseology speaks Peter on the day of Pentecost, Acts ii. 38, 39. " Be baptized " for the promise is to you and to your child-" ren." Hence Paul says that Abraham " re-" ceived the sign of circumcision, a seal of the " righteousness of the faith." It was an external sign of his faith in the promise of that seed, in whom he and all the seed of Israel should be the righteousness of God. Such is the promise,

in

in the faith of which Abraham and his seed were circumcised: and such is the promise in the faith of which we are Baptized. Hence the blessing or promise which we receive in Christ is called " the blessing of Abraham," to shew that circumcision and baptism stand upon the same promise.

3dly, The apostles and all that believed thro' their word knew very well, that the promise being to Abraham and his seed entitled his children to circumcision in infancy. In this case, it is easy to see, that since now they were commanded to extend the promise to all that should believe in all nations, they must necessarily conclude, that this promise extended equally to their children, so as to give them a title to baptism, the circumcision of Christ. Thus they must have concluded, unless there be found something in the commission prohibiting such a conclusion. But it is evident that the commission does not confine baptism to adults. It charges them to initiate the nations into his faith by baptizing them, just as Abraham was circumcised as a sign of his faith. Now by faith Abraham was not circumcised himself only, but also his infant-seed in consequence of his

his faith: confequently, fince there is nothing in the commiffion limiting baptifm more than circumcifion, it is impoffible that the apoftles fhould not conclude, that they were warranted to extend baptifm to the infants of believers, as well as to believers themfelves.—To this we may add

4thly, If the apoftles had not baptized the infant-feed of believers, the Jews would have certainly murmured at their conduct. They fet an high value on circumcifion. Even after they had believed in Chrift, they were weaned with much difficulty from a rite to which they had been fo long accuftomed. Many difputes this attachment gave birth to in the churches of Chrift. To allay thefe contentions, among other arguments adduced by Paul, he tells them that in Chrift we have the true circumcifion, even that of the heart; and alfo an external fign in baptifm of our connexion with Abraham, being the children of his faith, and fo heirs according to the promife. Now fuppofing baptifm to have been prohibited to their infant-children, they would not have failed to avail themfelves of this circumftance as invalidating the apoftle's argument. People fo tenacious of their

their antient rights, and so acute in finding objections against Paul's reasonings, would undoubtedly have employed an objection so powerful, and at the same time so obvious. The promise and its seal was given to Abraham's infant-offspring as well as to himself, but now you confine it to us, while our infants are considered as aliens and unclean, having no right to the promise or to the sign of that right. How, then, does baptism fill the place of circumcision?— Had the apostles prohibited infant-baptism, this objection would have certainly been produced by the Jews against their practice; and, in this case, we might surely have expected to find such an objection and its answer on record. But, as we have no hint of any such objection started in any part of the new testament writings, we have even reason to conclude, that none such was ever made, and consequently that there was no foundation for it in the apostolic practice.

If it be said, how came the apostles to baptize females, provided they viewed the law of circumcision as ascertaining the subjects of baptism, since no female was circumcised by the law of Moses. The answer is obvious. Soon

as

as the spirit taught them, that " there is neither " male nor female in Christ Jesus ;" or that christianity has levelled all such Distinctions among mankind, they must have known also that every sex has an equal title to baptism and all the other ordinances of the gospel. Had the female sex been denied baptism, there should still have been male and female in Christ Jesus. This, however, is but an extension of a right, not an infringement of it; and consequently could furnish no objection to such as were tenacious of it, as the prohibition of infant baptism would have done.—Female-baptism, too, was practised under the law.

5thly. Jesus had informed the apostles, before his death, that little children should be considered as members of the kingdom of God; and at the same time laid his hands on little children and blessed them. Now laying on of hands was a divine institution, a sign of conveying the spirit, or some blessing, the fruit of the spirit. When Jesus, therefore, laid his hands on little children and blessed them, he thereby shewed his apostles, that children were capable of receiving the spirit, and also of receiving a *visible sign* of their being members of the kingdom of God

God. In this case, when their master commanded his apostles to initiate the nations into his kingdom by baptism, it is impossible that they could consider infants as excluded from that right, or incapable of receiving the visible sign of admission to a kingdom, made up of little children, when they had heard their master declare that of such is the kingdom of God, and had seen him administer an ordinance to them expressive of this truth. They could not have interpreted the commission otherwise, unless it had expressly limited baptism to adults exclusive of their children, which it does not. If there be little children in the kingdom of God, it will be hard to show, why they may not receive the instituted sign of admission to that kingdom.

6thly, Every law, given to a people in general, is considered as binding the son as well as the father, infants and adults, provided it contains no exceptionary clause. This is the case all the world over. A king issues an edict for levying a tax on every subject of his kingdom. In this case subjects of every description must be supposed to be included; and so the tax-gatherers must necessarily explain the law. Had the king intended ed any particular class to be exeemed, he would have specified the class in this edict. The same may be said of an act granting a privilege to to the subject. If none be possitively excluded, all are supposed to be included. Thus we daily explain the acts of our British Parliament: and are the edicts of infinite wisdom dictated with less precision? To suppose this would be absurd. But in the law enjoining baptism no description of persons are excepted on account of age; and consequently all must be supposed to be included. This will be still more evident, if we observe,

7thly, That, in every system of law, children are considered as so connected with and included in their parents, that they have no separate existence as objects of law. Every where the son, while a child, enjoys every legal privilege in the right of his father; and if he transgress a law, the father only is amenable to justice for it. The son having no legal existence distinct from the father, law makes the parent responsible for the faults of the child as well as for his own.' Such are the laws of men: and such was the law of God given to Israel. The law given to the fathers included their children in all respects. The blessing and the curse extended to the fruit of their body as well as to their own persons. So says Moses, Deut. xxix. 10, 11, 12. "Ye stand this day all of you "before the Lord—All the men of Israel, your "little ones, your wives—That thou should-"est enter into covenant with the Lord thy "God," &c. Many of these little ones knew nothing of the matter; yet in the right of their parents they had a title to the promised blessings, and to circumcision, the instituted sign of this title. Thus they became a part of the holy nation, and had a right to be educated in the knowledge of the holy law. This is the foundation of these strong injunctions laid on the fathers in Israel, to "teach the commandments "of God diligently to their children." Deut. xvi. 6, 7. By circumcision they were bound to keep the law, which could not be done, without the knowledge of it. Hence the propriety of teaching them this knowledge.

Thus matters stood under the law of Moses, with respect to parents and children. Thus matters stood long before the law. Abraham and his seed were considered as one. The promise was to both; and both received the sign

of

of circumcision, the seal of the righteousness of faith in that promise, let us now see whether there be any hint in the new testament, whereupon we can establish a distinction between the believing parent and his seed, so as that the one is to be counted *holy*, and the other *unclean*.

When Peter called the Jews to repentance towards God and faith towards our Lord Jesus Christ, he exhorts them to be baptized. The reason he assigns is—" Because the promise is " to you, and to your children." This is the very language of the old testament—The language addressed to Abraham, when he and his seed were about to be circumcised. In this sense the Jews must undoubtedly have understood Peter, unless he had explained his words so as to exclude this sense: which he nowhere does.—Here it is vain to tell us that the word children does not always signify infants. This is incontestibly evident. But the question is whether the word children can have any other sense in this passage. Peter speaks to all, who were capable of hearing him and of understanding what he said. These he calls *you*. Now whom can he possibly mean by children of these hearers, but the infant-offspring which they ei-

H 2 ther

ther had or might have? So any messenger would be understood, who came, in the king's name, to proclaim that his master grants a certain priviledge to them that heard him and to their children. Is it possible that any could misinterpret this commission?—No more could we mistake the sense of Peter's embassy, were we unwarped by the prejudices of party.

Now if the promise being to the hearers be a reason for thus submitting to be baptized, it must also be a reason for baptizing the children; since the promise is said to be equally to both, and this is made the foundation of baptism. The baptists would make Peter a weak reasoner indeed. According to them, he says to his audience—" The promise is to you" therefore be ye baptized: the promise is also to your little ones, therefore let them not be baptized!—Spirit of party: What havock hast thou made of the scriptures!

To evade the force of the argument drawn from this text, Mr M'Lean pretends, that the promise here mentioned " is the promise of the " Holy Ghost spoken of by the prophet Joel, and not the promise given to Abraham and his seed." What a weak commentary is this! This

writer

writer himself admits, that Joel in that passage speaks of the spirit of prophecy, or the extraordinary and miraculous gifts of the Holy Ghost. Now these miraculous gifts were not conferred on all believers, even in the apostolic age, neither were they intended to be continued in the church in future periods. In this case, how could Peter give this promise as a ground and motive for submitting to baptism? If this be the promise which is to us and our children, in the faith of which christians are baptized, then baptism must either have been peculiar to the apostolic age, or all since that time have been baptized in the faith of a lie; since no such promise is accomplished to us now. I suppose the baptists themselves will not pretend that they have received an such gifts at their baptism. How, then, can they aver that the faith of receiving these gifts is the general foundation for baptism? The truth is, that promise in Joel had already its accomplishment, in the extraordinary effusion of the Spirit upon the apostles and disciples, Acts. ii. This Peter avers, and quotes the promise on purpose to prove his declaration: and consequently this is not the

the promise which is here said to be to all believers in all ages.

But if we take the promise here to intend all the saving influences of the spirit, then it is the very promise given to Abraham and his seed; for this promise of the spirit received by faith is expresly called " the blessing of Abraham, " which is come upon the Gentiles;" by which they become " heirs according to the promise." Gal. iii. 14. 29. It remains, then, that the promise to us and our children is the very promise given to Abraham, the promise of salvation by the seed, in whom all nations are blessed. This is the promise of which Peter speaks, as Mr M'Lean himself may see if he will read onwards to the 25 verse of the iii. chapter of the Acts—" Ye are the children of the promise, " and of the covenant which God made with " our fathers, saying to Abraham, and in thy " seed shall all the kindreds of the earth be " blessed." This is evidently the new covenant testament or promise, in which believers in all nations are concerned: and it is given to believers and their children as a foundation for baptism, just as it was given to Abraham and his infant-children as a foundation for circumcision cifion. Is it possible, then, that the Jews could understand Peter as saying any thing else, but that the promise of Abraham was to them and their infants and that both were under obligations to be baptized, just as Abraham and his children were under obligations to submit to circumcision, in testimony of his faith in the promise? It is certainly impossible they could have explained it otherwise, unless Peter had expresly told them that infants were excluded from baptism.

8thly, In this idea of connection between believing parents and their children Paul agrees with Peter. According to the law of Moses, an Israelite was not allowed to marry an heathen: or if any did so, he was commanded to put away his wife and the issue he had by her, as unclean or aliens from the commonwealth of Israel. Some members of the church of Corinth were in doubt, whether this law was still binding on Jews professing christianity. To this Paul answers, No such law is now in force, for "the unbelieving husband is sanctified to "the wife, and the unbelieving wife is sancti- "fied to the husband; else were your children "unclean, but now are they holy," 1. Cor. vii. 14.

14. Here the children of a believing parent are expressly called holy; and this holiness is said to be the result of their connection with such a parent. All who believed the promise made to Abraham were *separated* from the heathen, by that faith, to the service of the true God, before Christ came. This separation is called holiness: and this holiness extended to their seed no less than to themselves. Thus they were distinguished from the heathens, all of whom together with their seed, were called *unclean*, or common that is, lying in the common mass of mankind, not separated to the service of God by faith in the promised seed. This was the state of all the heathen then: this is their state still. These are the people Peter calls "common and unclean" in Acts x. Such is the sense of the word in the law of Moses. Now this holiness and uncleaness of the children is expressly said to be derived upon them from their parents. The Israelite believing the promise and obeying God begat a holy child: the heathen in unbelief begat a child unclean. Now Paul expressly says, that this is still the case under the gospel. The believing parent has an holy child. Nor is this impeded

impeded by his connexion in marriage with a heathen, for the marriage-connexion, the source of offspring, is now sanctified. The connexion is *holy*, although the unbeliever be *unclean*; the Mosaic law in question being now abolished, and marriage left on its original foot.—This says nothing about internal holiness. It is the holyness of which the law spoke: an external separation for the service of God, resulting from a profession of faith in the promise, or the gospel preached to Abraham, whether this profession was the offspring of the heart or of the mouth only. Whether *real* or *apparent* only, it intitled the man and his infant-offspring to church-membership, or to be considered as holy.

But it may be said, supposing that children are to be considered as holy in the sense mentioned, What argument can we draw from this in favour of infant-baptism? I answer, Paul says " now are they holy, *i. e.* now you treat them as holy. Now we know, that Israel of old treated their children as holy by circumcising them. Had they not done so, they would have used them as unclean. In what sense, then, could Paul say that the believing Corinthians

thians treated their children as holy, if they did not baptize them, or administer the sign of separation from the world to them, the instituted badge of church-membership? If they did not this, they certainly used them as unclean, or gave no evidence that they believed them to be holy.

Galled with this troublesome text, Mr McLean uses every effort to explain away its sense.—The holiness here meant, says he, is legitimacy. True, Sir; but not a legitimacy of the common kind. The offspring of Gentile-marriages were legitimate, yet still unclean. The legitimacy of the text, then, is the legitimacy of the marriage of an Israelite, when his marriage was lawful, the offspring was not only legitimate, or lawfully begotten, but they were holy, or entitled to be considered as separated to the service of God in the right of the parent. To tell a Jew, then, that his child is holy, is not only telling him that his son is lawfully begotten, but that he is holy or entitled to circumcision, the sign of church-membership. In the same manner, to tell a Jew believing in Christ that his children are holy, is to tell him that they have a right to baptism, the sign,
which

which is now the circumcifion of Chrift. So ftrong a connection has this text with infant-baptifm.

Again, he avers that " the holinefs of the " children here is of the fame kind with that of the unbelieving parents" \* becaufe their holinefs is inferred from the fanctification of the unbelieving parent. But how weak is this affertion! Paul calls the children holy, whereas the unbeliever is unclean, having no right to church-memberfhip. He does not fay that the unbeliever is holy: he only fays that the marriage-connection is holy, or that the unbelieving wife is fanctified in the *relation* fhe ftands in to the believing hufband. His connection with her is holy; not herfelf: whereas the children are exprefsly faid to be holy, in the law-fenfe of the word, that is, not ftrangers to, but connected with the holy covenant given to Abraham, feparating him and his feed from the heathen.

This argument may be farther illuftrated by an inftance taken from civil life. A Briton marries a Jewefs, who cannot inherit by the laws of his country. He doubts the legality of

his

---

\* Defence of believers baptifm, p. 46.

his marriage—whether his iffue by her can inherit. He is told, 'That although his wife cannot inherit either in her own perfonal right nor by any right he can give her, yet as the Britifh law does not prohibit his marrying a Jewefs, the marriage is Britifh, or fhe is *britainified* to him in that relation, fo that his iffue by her is confidered not as Jews but Britons, and fo can inherit the poffeffion of their father, according to law. The cafe is exactly in point: and in this cafe, it is eafy to fee, that the legitimacy of the child and that of the mother is not of the fame kind. The child is a Britifh fubject; fhe is not. The child can inherit, but fhe cannot —It is preceifely fo in the cafe before us. The child is holy, *i. e.* a member of the vifible church; the heathen mother is not. The child has a right to the privileges of the vifible church, while his mother has no title of that kind.

9thly, Agreable to the above view, chriftian parents are exhorted to bring up their children in the nurture and admonition of the Lord; and children to obey their parents *in the Lord*. Here, it is evident, both parents and children are confidered as in the Lord, or as chriftians, and fo bound to manifeft their fubjection to him

him by fulfilling their relative duties to one another, as the Lord hath enjoined. This is so obvious, that Mr M'Lean himself admits it. Here says he, " are exhortations to mutual " duties betwixt parents and children, even as " betwixt husbands and wives, masters and ser- " vants, &c." But to evade the argument commonly drawn from this, he adds, " the child- " ren here intended are not mere infants, but " believing children, visible members of the " churches, and capable of receiving and obey- " ing the word of exhortation."\* Let us see where this interpretation will lead us.—According to it, the children here addressed are visible members of the churches, and so of adult age, as none are visible members of the church but by baptism, which according to this hypothesis, is only administred to adults.—How ridiculous this idea! It supposes, 1st, That children are incapable of receiving either correction or instruction of a religious kind till they come to adult age and be baptized; 2dly, That parents are not bound by this injunction to bring up their children in the nurture and admonition of the Lord till they become adults; 3dly, That after we grow

---

\* Defence of beliver baptism. p. 75.

grow to men and women our parents are obliged to *bring us up* again, or to make us infants! These are the obvious consequences of this gentleman's interpretation. Yet, so inconsistent is error, he admits that " the gospel obliges christian pa-" rents to study the good of their children's " souls as well as of their bodies, to set a God-" ly example before them, and to instruct them " in the doctrines of the christian faith." Very just indeed. But are not the children at the same time obliged, by the same authority, to receive the instructions administered to them by the parents? If so, then they are under these obligations from the first moment, in which they are capable of receiving correction or instruction. Does Paul say that parents are *obliged* to instruct, while children are not *obliged* to receive their instructions? Does he not exhort both at the same time? or rather does he not begin with the duty of children?

The truth is; christian parents are hereby obliged to teach their offspring the doctrines of the Lord so soon as they are capable of such instruction: and as the Lord has commanded children to obey their parents, this must be early taught them soon as they believe this, they will

will obey their parents in the fear of the Lord. All this they may be taught even at two or three years of age, and in many instances sooner. Consequently even then they are supposed to be in the Lord as parents are commanded to deal with them as in the Lord, and they to obey in the Lord. Nor does it avail any thing to tell us, that " the apostles were commanded " to teach all nations the doctrine of the Lord, " while the nations were considered as *out of the* " *Lord.*" \* The scripture no where says that the nations were *in the Lord;* whereas the children in the above passages are considered as in the Lord as well as their parents. †

The characters and offices in Eph. vi. 1, 2. &c. will only apply to children under age. Adults are commanded to be kind to their parents but nowhere to obey them: nor can such be

I 2 viewed

---

\* Defence, &c. p. 74.

† A sensible friend on reading the above very judiciously asks—" Does it not merit regard in handling the argument from this text that the exortation stands in an epistle addressed to a gospel-church *as such?* Would not this evidently suppose the children there exhorted ( who in defiance of all quibble were children yet to be brought up) to have been understood as belonging to the *matter*, the *visible matter of* that Church ?"—I dare say every unbyassed mind will, answer in the affirmative.

viewed as the proper subjects of correction and instruction by parents *as such*. Only children in non-age can be trained or *brought up* by parents as such; they too are the proper subjects of parental chastisement and instruction. It is then evident as sun-shine, that infants and children under age are the objects of Paul's exhortation. These he considers as in the Lord, or holy. But holiness springs from the promise, which alone separates any person or thing for God. Consequently Paul views children as connected with the promise in which their parents have believed, else they would be unclean and not holy. Thus he establishes the doctrine of Peter—" The promise is to you and your " children." This is given as a reason of and motive to baptism. If so to the parents it must be so to the children.

But before we finish our examination of the apostolic commission to baptize, the following observations will add much weight to our interpretation of it as extending to infants. Baptism was no new institution. It was practised under the old testament. We have already seen, that the native Jews entered into the covenant or church of God by water. Every infant, male

and

and female, was baptized, or washed with water, in a religious view, soon after the birth. But we now add, that every proselyte from among the heathen to the faith of Abraham was admited into the church by baptism also. The *Talmud*, the *Gemara* and *Maimonides*, all agree, in respect of the manner of initiating both native Jews and proselytes. We shall only quote *Maimonides*, tit. *Isuri bia*. c. 13. *By three things the Israelites entered into the Covenant, by circumcision, baptism and sacrifice.* Again, *In all ages, whensoever any Gentile was willing to enter into the covenant, and to be gathered under the wings of the Shechinah, and to undertake the yoke of the law, he was bound to have circumcision, and baptism, and a peace offering (or as the gemara calls it the sprinkling of blood.) and if it were a woman, baptism and sacrifice.* He adds, *the stranger that is circumcised and not baptized, or baptized and not circumcised, is not truly a proselyte till he be both.*

From the above and many other testimonies, which might be quoted, it is evident, that all proselytes, male and female, were introduced to the Jewish church by baptism; and also, that the baptism of the native Jews was the *pattern* by which the baptism of proselytes was regulated, this practice was founded upon the law, Numb. xv. 15, 16. " one ordinance shall be both for you of the congregation, and for the stranger that sojourneth with you; an ordinance for ever in your generations: as ye are so shall the stranger be before the Lord. One law, and one manner shall be for you and for the stranger that sojourneth with you." By this law they considered themselves bound to receive proselytes by circumcision, baptism and sprinkling of sacrificial blood, as the Jews were entered into covenant by these three ordinances. Circumcision was instituted in the days of Abraham; baptism had been in use before his time: and when Israel were about to enter the covenant at Sinai they were not only baptized into Moses in the sea, but God, to prepare them for receiving the law, commands Moses—" Go unto the people, and sanctify them to-day and to-morrow, and let them wash their clothes." This *Maimonides* calls " baptism *Isuri bia*, c. 13. *Baptism was in the desert before the giving of the law, according as it is said, thou shalt sanctify them &c.* Then, finally, they were sprinkled with the blood of the covenant. Exod. xxiv. 8.

It

It muft be here obferved, that the infants of profelytes were alfo baptized, both male and female, in the fame manner as the infants of the native Jews were. fo fays the *gemara babyl. tit. chetub,* i. e. *They baptize the little or young ftranger or profelyte:* and the Gloffe adds that the *rulers of the confiftory take care of it, and fo are made to him a father.* So alfo *Maimonides,* in the forecited place, *they baptize the infant or little ftranger upon the knowledge or profeffion of the boufe of judgment.*

From the above detail the following obfervations naturally occur, 1ft, The apoftolic baptifm could not appear a novelty to the Jews nor even to the Gentiles, as baptifm had been a religious ceremony among all nations. Accordingly we no where read of any of them viewing it in that light. 2dly, Nor could the Jews object to the admiffion of profelytes to the covenant of Abraham by baptifm, as this had been fo long practifed by themfelves. Nor do we find them finding fault with this practice. They only objected to the admiffion of the Gentiles without circumcifion and a profeffed obligation to keep the law of Mofes. 3dly, In the commiffion mission to baptize our Lord had no occasion to specify the baptism of females. As this had been always practised in the church of God, the apostles must have understood their commission as extending to women, unless he had expressly limited it to men, as he did in enjoining circumcision. Accordingly, without any specific mention of women in their commission, their history informs that they administred baptism to both sexes indiscriminately. 4thly, Hence also we have the most certain foundation for infant-baptism in the christian church. As the infants of believing parents had been always admitted to baptism in the church of God before Christ came, proselytes to his religion must necessarily have demanded baptism for their children; nor could the apostles have possibly refused their request, unless their Lord had expressly prohibited them—a prohibition nowhere to be found. Indeed, nothing can be more evident than this, that Jesus never intended to change the subjects or mode of baptism in use before he came in the flesh. Had he intended any such alteration, he must undoubtedly have expressed his intention, and not have left his apostles in the dark in a matter of such importance;

portance; particularly as they muſt have baptized the infants of proſelytes without an expreſs prohibition, as this had been the univerſal practice in the church, wherein they had been educated, and that by divine appointment. 5thly, Hence alſo it is evident that baptiſm has not only kept the ſame place in the new teſtament ſtate of the church, which it held in the old, but that it has alſo ſuperſeded circumciſion and the ſprinkling of blood. We have ſeen that religious initiation was performed of old by a threefold ceremony, circumciſion, baptiſm and ſacrifice. Our Lord has choſen baptiſm to continue in his church, and alſo to anſwer all the purpoſe of the other two. This is the ſole ceremony which he has appointed in the initiation of diſciples into his church, and hence we can properly ſay that it has come in the room of circumciſion and the ſprinkling of blood, or has ſuperſeded them, and ſupplies their place in the church, of God under the goſpel. That it is called " the circumciſion of Chriſt is " clear from the paſſage above quoted. It is alſo " called the ſprinkling of the blood of Jeſus " Chriſt." Apoſtates from the faith of Chriſt are ſaid to " count the blood of the covenant " wherewith

"wherewith they were sanctified an unholy thing."* Sanctification here must mean baptism,

---

* Some interpreters think, that Christ, and not the apostate from christianity, is here said to be *sanctified* by the blood of the covenant Heb. x. 29. as they cannot allow apostates to have been sanctified, or purified from sin. But this objection originates in a mistake of the meaning of the word sanctification in this passage; wherein it can only mean an external dedication or *setting apart* of a person to the service of God. Even on their own hypothesis, this can only be its sense. Christ had no sin, and consequently could not be cleansed from it. When the father then is said to sanctify him and send him into the world, the meaning must be, he set him apart for his office: and when he is said to sanctifie himself, it means that he devoted himself to the service allotted him, by submitting to be sprinkled with the blood of his sacrifice, according to the law of the priesthood.—Again, the Hebrews knew perfectly the meaning of sanctification by the blood of the covenant; as their fathers had been so sanctified in the time of Moses, who took the blood and sprinkled it on all the people, saying, "this is the blood of the covenant, &c." Now that Paul, in the verse before us, refers to that transaction, I think it indisputably evident. This ascertains its sense. Moses was set apart to be mediator in the covenant at Sinai, before he entered on the office. Hence, he did not sprinkle the blood on himself, but "on the people." Paul, then, cannot mean, that Christ, acting as mediator of the better covenant, sprinkled the blood on himself, but "that he might sanctify the people, with his own blood, he suffered without the gate"

—Besides,

tifm, as in no other fenfe can apoftates be faid to have been fanctified. But this fanctification is by the blood of the covenant; and confequently the water in baptifm reprefents the blood of Jefus, and the act itfelf the fprinkling of that blood. Thus the true baptifm of Chrift not only "wafhes the body with pure "water," which was the part of the antient baptifm, but it alfo "fprinkles the heart from "an evil confcience," as the blood of the facrifical animal "fprinkled to the purifying of the flefh."

Having examined the apoftles' commiffion to baptize, and feen it extend to infants as well as adults, let us now proceed,

II. To examine the apoftolic practice with refpect to infant-baptifm. Here we fhall obferve.

1ft, That from the fhort hiftory we have of the adminiftration of baptifm by the apoftles there

—Befides, baptifm was always called fanctification by the Jews, as alfo by the chriftians for feveral centuries, as a vifible dedication to the fervice of God.—Finally, I cannot fee how a perfon can be faid to trample under foot and to profane a blood, which was never fprinkled upon him, or with which he had no connection.—Thefe reafons determine me to think that it is the apoftate, who is here faid to have been fanctified, *i. e.* fprinkled with the blood of the covenant in baptifm.

there arises the highest degree of probability that they baptized infants as well as adults. We read of their baptizing whole households: Lydia, for instance, and her household; the Jaylor, and all that were his; and the household of Stephanus. Now is it probable, or even credible, that in all the households baptized there was not one child? And supposing that there was an infant in any of these families, and the infant excluded from baptism, we might certainly have expected to find this on record; particularly as this would have been an entire novelty in the church of the living God. For many hundred years, even from the days of Abraham, infants had had a place in the visible church, by divine appointment. Had they been now excluded from this station, and cast out into the heathen world, so great a change would certainly have been particularly marked in the scriptures. Nothing less than a divine law could exclude infants from this privilege; and if any such law had been made, it must have been recorded in some part of the sacred records. It must be found either in the words or practice of the apostles. The silence of the new testament, then, on this head renders it

evident

evident that no such law ever existed. 2dly. The uniform practice of the primitive churches, immediately succeeding the apostolic age, affords evidence on this point amounting, in my apprehension, to a certainty. Such as lived in so early a period as the first, second and third centuries, undoubtedly have known what was the practice of the apostles themselves; and as the churches in these periods remained, in a great measure, uncorrupted by innovations and superstitions, no change of that practice could have taken place without very considerable opposition. Or if some churches had deviated in this respect, it is incredible that the whole would have so early apostatized from the original institution. But the writers of these times not only attest that infant-baptism was practised in their times, but some of them expresly declare, that it was the practice of the apostles themselves. Did their testimony, indeed, contradict any thing said in the sacred oracles, it is totally inadmissible, but since it corresponds so exactly with every suggestion of scripture, we cannot reject it unless we chuse to say what would tend to invalidate the authenticity of the scriptures themselves—that the primitive churches were all liars.

We might produce a large cloud of witnesses in proof of this point—even all the writers of the first seven centuries. But as these have been all produced in evidence by other writers on this subject, I shall only mention a very few.

Justin Martyr wrote his 2d apology about the year 148, in which he says, there were christians then living, some seventy years old, who had been made disciples to Christ from their infancy, and therefore must have been baptized in the first age, while some of the apostles were living. He also calls baptism the spiritual circumcision, as succeeding the circumcision in the flesh.

Irenæus Bishop of Lyons, born about the year 97, a disciple of Polycarp, who was a disciple of John the Divine, and so could not be mistaken about the practice of the churches down to his time, expressly mentions the baptism of infants. As baptism is the outward sign of regeneration, it is called by him and many others regeneration, the thing signified put for the sign, by an usual figure in scripture. " When " Christ" says he, " gave his disciples the com-

" mand

"mand of regenerating unto God, he said—
"Go and teach all nations, baptizing them, in
"the name of the Father, and of the Son, and
"of the Holy Ghost." To which he adds,
"Christ came to save those, who by him are
"regenerated unto (God *i. e.* baptised,) both
"infants and little ones, and young men and
"elderly persons."

Origen was born about the year 183 within 100 years of the apostles. Both his father and grandfather were christians. He was one of the most learned men of that age, and had preached the gospel in Rome, Greece, Palestine and Syria, and so could not but be acquainted with the usages of all the churches. This great author expressly declares infant-baptism to have been in constant use in the churches. "The baptism of children," says he, "is gi-
"ven for the remission of sins." This he says, while proving the doctrine of original sin in his eight homily: And in his comment on the Romans he expressly says that infant-baptism was derived from the themselves apostles.

Tertullian, contemporary with Origen, has been often adduced by the baptists in proof of their side of the question: whereas he furnishes us with the strongest evidence that infant-baptism was the uniform practice of the church in his day.

It is true, he speaks against it in common cases, and advises that it should be delayed till grown to years, yea, till after marriage. The reason was, because he had a notion that sins committed after baptism were next to, if not utterly unpardonable: hence he advised the delay of the baptism of children, unless in case of necessity, till married, imagining they would then be less liable to temptation. This evidently proves that infant-baptism was the practice of the church. If it was not so, why should he speak against it? Surely he would not fight with his own shadow, or oppose a custom that had no existence. Besides, he did not say infant-baptism was unlawful, as he allowed it in case of necessity, *i. e,* when the child was in danger of death, and only disapproved of it for the absurd reason abovementioned.

The writings of Ambrose, Austin and other fathers have been produced in this argument, who expressly tell us that infant-baptism had been ever in use from the time of the apostles. But I shall only produce farther the testimony

of

of Pelagius, who in the fifth century denied original sin. In anfwer to him, Auftin infifts on the baptifm of infants, which was the known and ftanding practice of the churches, as an argument of their natural defilement. "Infants," fays he, "are by all chriftians acknowledged to "ftand in need of baptifm, which muft be in "them for original fin, fince they have no o-"ther." Pelagius was much puzzled with this argument, yet does not deny that infants fhould be baptized. So far from this, when fome charged him with fuch denial as the neceffary confequence of his doctrine, he repells the charge thus —" Men flander me, as if I denied bap-"tifm to infants; whereas I never heard of a-"ny, not the worft of heretics, that would fay "fuch a thing of infants."

Upon this Mr Boftwick, in his fermon on infant-baptifm, very juftly obferves.—'This con-'feffion is the ftrongeft demonftration, that infant-baptifm was univerfally practifed, time out of mind, or elfe he, whofe intereft it was to deny it, to anfwer the arguments of his adverfary, would certainly have done it. But fo far is he from that, though his caufe required it, he exprefsly declares, he does not deny it, nor ever

ever heard of any that did. Now Pelagius was a great scholar and a great traveller. He had been at Rome, Africa, Egypt, and Jerusalem, where he spent much time, and therefore must have been acquainted with the rites of the fathers, and customs of the churches in all those parts; and yet he declares that he had never heard of any that denied baptism to infants. It is as plain then as history can make it, that there had been then no dispute about the point; and that there was not, neither had been any sect professing christianity, that denied it, from the apostles' time to that day. Nor is there the least evidence, that it was ever opposed by any man or society of men, for a long time after. The consequence, then, is, If infant-baptism be a nullity, and not Christ's institution, then the churches lost an ordinance of Christ during all this period. Nay, they must have lost it in the very first ages and purest times, and there must have been no regular baptism, no christian ministers or ordinances for so many centuries. Many adults were indeed baptized during that period; some of whom might become ministers of the word; but they baptized

tized infants, and consequently were not christians, according to the view of the baptists.

Again, if infant-baptism had, in any of these periods, been introduced by men, and had not been the custom of the church from the apostles; how strange is it, that we have no account, no not the least hint, in all antiquity, when, or by whom it was introduced? Had it been human invention, would it have been so universal in the first 300 years, and yet no record left, when it was introduced nor of any dispute or controversy about it? This is incredible.

It may be added, since no man has authority to baptize, who has not been baptized himself, and a regular succession of adult baptisms cannot be pretended, how, then, can any man, with a good conscience join the present baptists? All the present adult baptisms, if traced back, must come originally from those, who were baptized in infancy, and consequently, on their principles, can have no validity in them. Since, then, no man can be esteemed a christian, who has not received Christ's baptism, visible christianity must perish for ever, unless Christ shall send us apostles to baptize us again. In short,

short, on the baptist plan, there neither is, nor can be a church of Christ on earth.

The above quotations from the fathers are not produced to determine whether infant-baptism be an institution of Christ or not; but to ascertain a matter of fact, viz. that infants have been baptized in all the churches of Christ from the days of the apostles to their times. Of this they must be allowed to be competent judges; and consequently the fact stands indisputably evident.

The sum of the argument for infant-baptism stands thus—From the days of Abraham, by divine appointment, infants had been admitted into the church of the living God, by a sign common to infants and adults.—In the new testament a sign of the same intention is appointed, while we have not the obscurest hint of the exclusion of infants from this privilege, either in the appointment itself or in the apostles' reasoning on that subject or in their consequent practice—On the contrary, the apostles seem to explain their commission to baptize as extending to infants as well as adults, considering them as holy, and addressing them as in the Lord, when born of believing parents.—Nor is

there

there any hint of the Jewish believers objecting to the apostles practice in this matter; which they would certainly have done, had they paganized their children—Add to all this, that the whole history of the most ancient churches of Christ tends to establish the fact, that infant-baptism was practised in the apostolic churches—All which taken together afford such a high degree of evidence to the divinity of this institution as amounts to a certainty.

Thus we have proved that infants were admitted into the church of God, and never have been excluded so far as we can see by any divine appointment. It is the task, then, of the baptists to prove that they have been so excluded, otherways their argument is destitute even of the shadow of a probability.

## SECT. IX.

*Containing* ANSWERS *to the* OBJECTIONS *of the* BAPTISTS.

That we may judge with more precision in this matter we must hear counsel on the other side.

I. The baptists derive their chief argument from

from the commission itself—" Go, disciple all nations, baptizing them:" telling them " He that believeth and is baptized shall be saved." The nations must first be taught and profess their faith in the gospel, ere they can be baptized, according to this law; and hence it is concluded that the law excludes infants from this sacred rite. A mighty stress has been laid on this argument: let us see how far it can bear it. When God sent Moses to deliver Israel from Egypt, he commanded him to preach a gospel, the good news of deliverance, to them; telling them, that whoever kept the passover and the sprinkling of blood in faith of salvation from the destroyer should be delivered. In consequence of this faith they " were " all baptized into Moses in the cloud and in " the sea." Hence, the baptists, if they will keep by their argument, must necessarily conclude, that all the infants of Israel were left in Egypt. They could not understand Moses nor profess the faith by keeping the passover and the sprinkling of blood, more than our infants now can hear and believe the apostolic gospel. Moses, too, was only commanded to preach to them that were capable of hearing and understanding

standing what he said: consequently no infant could lawfully be baptized into Moses! Again, When Moses gave this law at Sinai, he said, "Hear o Israel,—Thou shalt love the Lord thy God, &c." Thus the law or covenant was addressed to adults, such as could hear and understand him, and say, "All that the Lord has spoken we will do, and will be obedient." In testimony of this faith, they had the blood of the covenant sprinkled on them, or they were baptized—"Moses took the blood of the covenant sprinkled it on all the people," or on the twelve pillars representing all the tribes. Had the baptists lived then, they would certainly have argued, that this covenant did not include infants, as there is no word of sprinkling any but such as professed faith in and obedience to the law given in consequence of their hearing it preached. Yet nothing can be more evident, than this, that the covenant was not made with them only, who were taught the law but with their little ones also.

The truth is, every law is addressed immediately to adults; yet every man living in subjection to that law, considers his children as under the same law, and trains them up in that idea.

idea. Thus Israel were commanded to teach the law of God diligently to their children, viewing them as bound by that law; thus also christian parents are charged to train up their children in the nurture and admonition of the Lord, that from their childhood they might know the scriptures,—evidently supposing that the children were bound to obey them.

If it be still urged, that faith is always considered as a necessary prerequisite to baptism; we answer, faith was always a prerequisite to admission into the covenant of God and to the sign of such admission. It was as necessary under the law as under the gospel. Such as kept the passover by faith in the divine promise of deliverance from destruction in Egypt, were baptized into Moses in the cloud and in the sea. Such as believed the promise of Canaan, and promised a corresponding obedience, were sprinkled with the blood of the covenant. The blessings of that covenant were promised only to such as believed. Only the believer entered into the promised rest. Others could not enter in because of unbelief. Abraham, too, believed God before he was circumcised, or received the seal of the righteousness of the faith. Yet is it not certain

certain that the children of these believers, even infants incapable of believing, enjoyed all these promises and received the signs or seals of them, as well as their parents? how weak, then, is it to argue, that infants can have no visible interest in, or title to the sign of a covenant while incapable of believing. Faith is only required of adults. This was as strictly required under the old testament as under the new. If the want of it, then, exclude infants now from the sign of the covenant, it must have done so formerly.

Yet every initiation of a child into the church of God proceeded on the foot of a profession of faith in the divine promise, on which the church was founded. Abraham professed this faith, and hence, as a sign of it, circumcised his infant, Isaac as well as himself. If any Israelite forsook the faith his child had no title to circumcision. The case is so still with respect to baptism.

But, says Mr M'Lean, if infant baptism rests on the faith of the parent, we must be sure our parents were believers ere we can be sure that we have received christian baptism.* D'Anvers says the same thing: and a weak saying it is.

L It

* Defence, &c. p. 81.

It equally militates against adult-baptism. How many have the baptists dipped who never *really* believed? Does this render their baptism unchristian? If not, no more can it render our baptism of none effect, whether the faith of our parents was real or professed only.

2dly, The baptists demand of us either precept or example for infant-baptism; neither of which, say they, can be found in scripture. To this we reply, We have clearly proved that infants were initiated into the church of God, by all the rites of divine institution for that purpose, from Abraham to Christ. Even the children of proselytes were circumcised and baptized. Now as Christ, when he commanded his apostles to baptize, did not exclude infants, they must undoubtedly be included in the commission. Had he intended to alter the law and practices of baptism, so universal in the Jewish church, he would have certainly specified the alteration in the commission itself. But as no such thing can be found in the commission, the apostles must have proceeded to administer baptism, not only to every proselyte but to every infant of a proselyte to the faith of their master, as this had been the practice of the church of God

God in all past ages. This being the case, we have no occasion for express examples of infant-baptism. every proselyte to the faith of Christ would unavoidably ask this privilege for their infants, nor could the apostles refuse to grant it, as their master had nowhere prohibited them. Accordingly they speak of the infants of believers as *in the Lord* and *holy*—titles never given to any but to such as had received the sign of initiation into the holy covenant. This ascertains the apostolic practice in this matter.—It belongs, then, to the baptists to prove that our Lord prohibited the baptism of infants, or that the apostles refused to baptize them. Till they do this, which I can venture to say they never will, infant baptism stands on the most incontrovertable evidence. *

---

* Since this Dissertation went to the press I have read Mr. M'lean's new performance, entitled, The *Nature and Import of baptism.* In p. 2. he says, " As baptism is an in-
" stitution peculiar to the new and better covenant, so it is
" to be found in that book called the new testament, or
" covenant, and there only." Then he proceeds to charge all, who would look for any thing relating to this institution in the old testament, as having " something else in their
" view than the simple institution of Christ." Strange assertions these! I hope my reader will find the contrary clearly

3dly, They pretend that baptism can be of no use to infants as they are incapable of understanding its

ly proved in the above sheets.—I now add, Did not John baptize? Was his baptism *peculiar* to the new covenant, or, in other words, to the new testament church?—Again, the word *church* " is to be found in that book called the " new Testament, and there *only*" must we not, then, on this gentleman's principles, conclude, that a church " is an in- " stitution peculiar to the new and better covenant," and that there was no church under the old testament? If so, will it not also follow, that this gentleman, who finds a church in the old Testament, containing all that is essential to the constitution of a society of that kind, must " sure have some- " thing else in his view than the simple institution of Christ?" So fairly do his own words condemn him!—Commentators too frequently take the liberty to differ from Paul in *Sentiments*, but generally take care not to contradict him in *express terms*. This author, howbeit, is not so *delicate*. Paul expressly says—The law stood " in diverse baptisms." No says Mr M'Lean; there is no such institution as baptism " to be found in the old testament!"

In the preface to this new work, it is observed that " the " controversy seems now to be pretty much exhausted, there " being little published on that subject of late years but a " repetition of former arguments." It must be owned, this author has taken care to verify this assertion in his present work, as there is not one sentiment, argument or the shadow of an argument to be found in it, relating to the subject or mode of baptism, which this author *himself* has not published before, particularly in his defence of believer-baptism."

its import and design.—This objection is a replying against God, who commanded infants to be admitted into his church by circumcision. Infants can understand the import and design of baptism as well as the infants of old understood the intention of circumcision, baptism and the sprinkling of blood. I add, *laying on hands* was a divine ordinance, and is put on a level with baptism, Heb. vi. 2. But Jesus laid his hands on infants and blessed them; though they understood not the import of that action. How inconclusive, then, is this argument of the Baptists! It only displays their own ignorance. Baptism entitles infants to the care of the church—to be educated in the nurture and admonition of the Lord. Thus they are secured during nonage against ignorance, error, and idolatry—a privilege of the highest importance.

4thly, It is argued, That this practice confounds the church with the world, making the birth of the flesh entitle one to a place in

tism." New writers must have new readers; and a new arrangement of argument may give additional weight to the argument: but it is hard to see for what purpose the *same* author re-publishes the *same* ideas, without so much as attempting to engage attention afresh by at least a diversification of expression.

the kingdom of God. A senseless objection this! Did circumcision and baptism of old confound the church with the world? Or rather, was it not the very badge of distinction between believers and heathens? It was so, while in nonage; but if, when children arrived at riper years, they turned aside from the true God to idols, the were cut off from the congregation of the Lord, as heathens. In this case they shewed that they were not Jews; for he never was a Jew, who was one outwardly. It is so still. Soon as any baptized in infancy shakes off the profession of the faith of Jesus, or denies it in practice, that soul is to be cut off from his people, as a heathen man and publican.

Had this argument any weight, it is of equal force against adult baptism. In both ways, hypocrites are blended with true believers. Simon Magus was of the world; yet he received adult baptism. Did this confound the church with the world? No: soon as his hypocrisy appeared, he was cast out of the church. He would have shared the same fate, had he been baptized in infancy.

Nor does infant-baptism proceed on the supposition, that the birth of the flesh entitles one

to

to a place in the kingdom of God. The fleshly birth never conferred such a claim. It did not so even in the national kingdom of Israel. Abraham believed God, and then was circumcised with his seed. In like manner, every Jew professing the faith of Abraham had a title to circumcision for his child. But soon as any Jew despised or disbelieved the promise, he was no more considered as a Jew himself, nor had his infant-seed any title to circumcision. The children of the flesh never were the children of God: only the children of the promise, or such as professed faith in the promise, were counted for the seed. Many of Israel fell short of the kingdom of Canaan. Why? Were they not Abraham's fleshly seed? Yes: but they were not the children of his faith: They could not enter in because of " unbelief." Soon as Esau despised the birth-right, neither he nor his seed had any title to circumcision, or to a place in the kingdom of Canaan. While the parent continued in the faith, his child was considered as of the same faith, and so had a title to circumcision, the seal of the righteousness of the faith. The case is precisely the same now. Not a connexion with a parent as of the flesh, but a connection with a parent as of the faith, can entitle a child to a place in the visible kingdom of Jesus Christ.—In short, no objection can be brought against infant-baptism but is equally strong against infant-circumcision.

5thly, The argument taken from circumcision will excite the sneer of the baptists. They tell us, circumcision was a sign of the old covenant, the seal of a right to an earthly inheritance and temporal privileges, intended to distinguish the fleshly seed of Abraham, to which one had a claim by his birth of the flesh; whereas baptism is a sign of the new covenant, a sign of spiritual and heavenly blessings, to which no man is born heir by his natural birth: and consequently we cannot infer the right of infants to baptism, from the right they had to circumcision.—This is the leading error of the baptists, involving in it a vast number of mistakes of no small importance, and of consequence it requires a very minute discussion: but as such an investigation would fill a too disproportionate department in this Dissertation, I have reserved it for a separate publication, announced in the preface to this small performance.—In the mean-time, the argument taken from the
admission

admission of proselytes with their infants by baptism under the law, in support of the continuance of that practice under the gospel, stands inviolably firm, secured against the keenest attacks of the enemy.

6thly, The argument derived from the practice of infant-baptism in the first christian churches after the apostolic age has been strongly opposed. Baptists have denied the fact although the truth of it be supported by such incontestible evidence that it must seem amazing how any could ever presume to call it in question. To invalidate the evidence, they have pretended to produce a variety of instances of children born of christian parents, who were not baptized when young: but this is a mere assertion, unsupported by even the shadow of proof. Many eminent fathers in these churches were not baptized till they arrived at manhood, but it cannot be proved that their parents professed christianity at the time of their birth: and even although this could be proved, it would conclude nothing with respect to the general practice of the churches, as will be evident to all, who attend to the many false and whimsical ideas, which got possession of the minds of

many

many members of these churches in a pretty early period. It will be worth while to trace these ideas, particularly as among them we will easily find

### The ORIGIN of the BAPTISTS.

We have already seen, that the famous *Tertullian* had adopted a fancy, that every sin committed after baptism was either unpardonable or nearly so; for which reason he earnestly recommended the delay of baptism till at least the heat of youthful passion subsided. Now as *Tertullian* was a man of such eminence in his time, we may be sure that an advice from him, urged with vehemence, and supported by such plausible arguments, could not fail to influence many. This was also a leading opinion among the sect called *Novatians*; in consequence of which infant-baptism could not be practised among that sect: and I may add nor adult-baptism either till the hour of death, as they denied the remission of sins to christians, sinning after baptism.

Others again imagined, that the very act of baptism washed away all sin whatever, and hence deferred baptism that every one might gratify

his

his lusts without restraint, knowing that, if he could get himself baptized before death, he was sure of a full remission.—Others would delay baptism till they had attained the thirtieth year, because Christ was baptized at that period of life. On a similar pretence, *Constantine* the great would not be baptized but in the river Jordan; and hence as he never came to that place, he only submitted to baptism on his death-bed. Some moreover, deferred baptism till they could have access to be baptized by some eminent Bishop.—All these opinions and refutations of each of them are to found in the writings of *Bazil, Gregory Nazianzen, Chrysostom, Augustine's confession,* and *Eusebius life of Constantine.*

From the above short detail, it is easy to see what a powerful and extensive influence these ideas must have exerted among mankind—ideas suited to the taste of the whimsical, the capricious, the fond of novelty, the lovers of pleasure; supported at the same time by men of talents, in eminent stations, and renowned for piety and learning. Seeds so congenial to the soil of man, and cherished with so much care, must have taken such a firm hold of the human heart, that we need not wonder if time itself has

has not been able to extirpate them. Had they not been checked in their progress by the strenuous efforts of men of great eminence in the churches, they would probably have overspread the far greater part of the christian world. The votaries of these opinions, howbeit, still mantained a footing in various places; and although for a long time they seem to have inculcated the delay of baptism for such reasons as have been mentioned, yet, as the transition from these to an absolute denial of the divine authority for infant-baptism was so very easy, in process of ages, infants were excluded from baptism altogether, and that as is usual, in the name of Jesus Christ. When or where this last idea had its birth, I imagine cannot be ascertained. It seems to have dwelt in obscurity for a time, till at last it burst forth from its solitude in the sixteenth century, and made a very considerable progress in Germany, extending its influence to Holland, Britain and other countries; in all which it still maintains its ground.—Thus it has assumed various forms. At first it deferred the baptism of infants on prudential considerations; at last it divested them of their right, and made the sacred oracles pronounce against them the sentence of exclusion. In all stages, however, it seems unhappily to have laid a disproportionate stress on what the schoolmen call the *opus operatum*, the act itself and the mode of performing it. A finger undipped would render baptism of no effect! Would make it " a mere human ordinance!" Scripture too must be called in to support this fancy.—What has not been spoken and done in the name of the Lord?—False ideas in religion, it seems, must still be

THE MAGGOTS OF CORRUPTED TEXTS,

M

# AN ENQUIRY INTO THE LAWFULNESS OF EATING BLOOD.

GOD and men view things in very different lights. What appears important in our eye is very often of no account in the estimation of infinite wisdom; and what appears trifling to us is often of very great importance with God. It was so from the beginning. The disputer of this world cannot see any thing worthy so severe a punishment, in eating the fruit of the forbidden tree: yet through this offence by the divine determination, sin and death, with all their attendant woes, came into the world. The next prohibition we read of, with respect to food, is found annexed to the grant of animal food to man, Gen. ix. The Sovereign proprietor, when he gave us a grant to eat of the flesh of our fellow-animals, gave it with this reservation or limitation.—" The flesh " with the blood thereof, that is the life there- " of, thou shalt not eat of it." Against this, also, as an unreasonable and trifling prohibition, the wisdom of this world has often declaimed, or, by shameful evasions and idle quibbles, has explained away the sense of the divine mandate, that the conscience of the creature might be furnished with an apology for transgressing the law of its master. Yet this same precept was retained and strongly enforced in the law given to Israel from Sinai; while the breach of it was guarded against by the most awful sanctions. Yea, even under the gospel, it seemed meet to the holy spirit speaking in the apostles to enjoin the observation of this law on all the disciples of Jesus Christ. Acts xv. It is allowed on all hands that this decree was in force at least to the time of the final destruction of Jerusalem by the Romans: but if it shall be found, by searching the scriptures, that it was intended by the holy spirit to continue in force to the end of the world, how faulty shall the many be found,

found, who consider the observance or non-observance of it as a matter of indifference? Now as disputes on this point have run high, and many arguments have been offered on both sides of the question, it must concern every christian to examine what is offered from the scriptures by both parties, that he may either eat or forbear to eat blood in faith, or from a conviction of Christ's authority for his conduct; since Paul assures us, "he that doubteth is condem-"ned if he eat; since whatsoever is not of "faith is sin."

Entering on this subject it is proper we should observe, that as the Creator is the sovereign proprietor and lord of all things, no creature can have any independent right to any thing whatever. Life, and consequently all the means of supporting it, must be derived from the great author of our being. Man, in particular, as a moral agent, amenable to his maker for every part of his conduct, must live by every word that proceeds out of the mouth of God; or by such means as God has granted for supporting his life; and any attempts to live in another way, or by other means than God has revealed to him, is the higheſt act of rebellion againſt the univerſal Lord.

It will be alſo allowed, That when God gave man a right, grant, or title to eat of any particular ſpecies of food, he might at the ſame time give it under reſervation or limitation, retaining a part of that ſpecies of food in his own power, and prohibiting man from eating of it under certain penalties marked in the grant. In this caſe, abſtinence from the part prohibited is, on man's part, an acknowlegement of his dependance on his ſovereign for the part granted; or that he has no original independent claim either to life or the means of its ſupport.

Having theſe points in view we muſt look into the ſacred records, that we may ſee what creature God has granted us a right to eat; and with what reſervation the grant is given.

There are only two grants of this kind recorded in ſcripture the firſt is to be found in the firſt chapter of Geneſis, containing a right given to man to eat of the vegetable creation, or of every green herb: the ſecond is recorded in the ninth chapter of that book, and contains a title granted to man to eat of the inferior animals. Of both theſe kinds then it is lawful for man

man to eat, till his sovereign be pleased to reverse the grant. Both grants, however, contain a reservation with penalties annexed; the first of a species of vegetable, called the tree of knowledge of good and evil; the second, of the blood, the life of the animal. This last grant contains a renewal of the former. Gen. ix. 3. " Every moving thing that liveth shall be meat " for you: even as the green herb have I given " you all things." This grant was given to all mankind then in being, by them to be conveyed down to their posterity, and consequently all nations are interested in this grant, which is made irreversible by the granter as he has established it " to perpetual generations," (Gen. ix. 12.) in token of which, he has given us " the bow in the cloud."

One would be apt to conclude from the avowed irreversibility of this charter or grant, that the reservation it contains must be equally irreversible with itself; or that so long as man partakes of animal food, he should eat it with the reservation of the blood, so expressly specified in the charter, authorizing him to eat of the flesh. Particularly, this would appear to be of vast consequence to man, since it would

appear

appear that on this condition only, God has promised to have respect to the blood of man by requiring it at the hand of the shedder. " The blood thou shalt not eat: " And the blood of " *your* lives will I require" &c. \* Gen. ix. 4, 5, 6. This would seem to say that God will pay no regard to the life of that man, who does not forbear to eat the blood or life of the inferior animals.

This grant with its reservation was given to all men, and has been conveyed down to all ages and generations both of Jew and Gentile; to the former by a written, to the latter by an unwritten tradition. So that no man whatsoever can lawfully eat blood, or eat it but at the expence of his own life, or of forfeiting his right to the atonement for his soul, unless he shall find in the sacred oracles a reversal of this reservation by the hand that gave us the original charter; or, in other words, that God has contradicted himself, by reversing a deed, which he himself has declared to be established to perpetual generations.

It is admitted by all, that this grant with its
reservation

---

\* This certainly means, that if we eat blood, he will not require the blood of our lives. I see not how it can read otherwise.

reservation was in full force, during the mosaic dispensation, as it is taken into the Jewish law; where it is renewed in the strongest terms, and forms an essential part of that code. Lev. xvii. Nor did it bind the Jews only, as is generally imagined, but extended its obligation to the Gentile also. That no stranger, sojourning among the Jews, was allowed to eat blood is clear from Lev. xvii. 10, 12, 13. Nor was the observation of this law of small importance. So far from it, the most dreadful imprecation was pronounced against the transgressor: "What-"soever man there be of the house of Israel, "or of the stranger that sojourneth among you, "that eateth any manner of blood, I will even "set my face against that soul that eateth blood, "and will cut him off from among his people." Nor was it less criminal for the Gentiles in other countries to eat blood. Hence David speaks of their practice with abhorrence Ps. xvi. 4. "Their drink-offerings of blood will I not of-"fer." This refers to the practice of the Syrians, who made libations of blood to their gods; and prophetically to the antichristian idolaters, who offer the literal blood of our sacrifice in the cup of the mass. Yet the Gentiles

tiles feem not in general to have made blood a common meal: only, as the doctrine of atonement by blood was among the things which God fhewed to all men, it was eafy for a vain imagination to conclude that the blood of a facrifice was proper to be offered in drink-offerings, as moft acceptable to the Gods. Thus their error was much more excufable than that of chriftians, fince it originated in a religious veneration for the blood of atonement.

Let us now fee how this grant ftands in the new teftament, that we may know whether the granter, the lord of life, has freed us from the obligation the grant lays us under, as the tenure or holding by which we have a title to eat flefh, and to expect an atonement for our lives. And here it is certainly of importance to obferve; that at the fame time, when the Holy Ghoft by the apoftles declares the Gentiles free from the yoke of circumcifion, and fo from the whole ritual law, he enforces the obligation of the law, enjoining abftinence from blood-eating, as a neceffary thing; yea, no lefs fo than abftaining from idolatry and fornication. Acts. xv. Nor have we the leaft hint of a reverfal of that

that decision any where in any after-part of new testament scripture.

If, then, man forfeited his title to life, or, what is the same thing, to the food which supports it, by eating the fruit of the tree, reserved in the proprietor's hand by the first charter or grant of vegetable food; one would be apt to conclude, that the same consequence must follow on his eating blood, as abstaining from eating it is made the express tenure by which he holds his right to eat flesh and to have an avenger of the blood of his own life. The scripture informs us, that the first forfeiture was owing to the subtilty of satan; nor can the second be ascribed to any other original. The first stratagem succeeded by a misinterpretation of the terms of the original grant; and when we examine the following arguments, produced in favours of blood-eating, we may perhaps find that mankind have been deceived into the second forfeiture by an artifice of the same kind.—Let us examine them and see.

1st, It is argued, that the distinction between clean and unclean meats is abolished in Christ; therefore every kind is clean to the Christian.— Very true, friend: but ere this argument can hold

hold in favours of blood-eating, you must prove, first, that blood was given to man for meat; and, secondly, that it is classed among the unclean meats in the Mosaic system. In Lev. xi. and Deut. xiv. Chapters we have a full list of the unclean meats. There the eagle, the vulture, the raven, &c. are called unclean; but not a syllable concerning blood. Again, when blood is prohibited as meat, it is forbidden not because it is unclean, but because it is *precious* being the life of all flesh; and because it is *holy* being the atonement or ransom of the soul. Since, then, blood never was given to man for meat; and even when eating it is prohibited, it is not called unclean but holy, it is plain, that a law, making unclean meats clean, cannot affect the law concerning blood, which is not classed among meats at all, much less among the unclean. The gospel had no occasion to make clean, what the law had already pronounced holy.—How absurd thy glosses on scripture, O serpent! Yet how powerful their influence on the mind of the simple!

Moreover, this argument goes on the supposition that there is no meat called unclean under the gospel; whereas it is obvious, that I-
dolothytes

dolothytes or meats offered to idols, when eat in the idols temple, are as unclean as ever, as by eating them christians incur the most awful punishments, Rev. ii. 14, 16, 20, 21, 22, 23.

2dly, Blood under the law was a figure of the blood of Christ; therefore, say the advocates for blood-eating, the precept concerning it was not moral, but ceremonial, and so ceased with other shadows when Christ the substance came. This argument is founded upon a double mistake: 1st, It supposes, that no precept of a moral or lasting obligation can be a figure or shadow of Christ and his church. This is false in fact. The law of God enjoining marriage, Gen. 2d and 9th chapters, is undoubtedly moral, given to all men for all ages; yet Paul assures us, Eph. v. that it was a type of the union between Christ and his church. Will any aver, that now Christ has come and married his church and had children begotten by the word of truth, therefore marriage is no more a duty? 2dly, But the principal mistake this argument is built on, and which all writers on this subject have inadvertently gone into, is, That the blood of beasts in general was a figure of the blood of Christ. No idea can be more wide of the truth.

Only the blood of the sacrifical animals was so; whereas the blood of beasts slain for common use is no where said to be typical. Hence when God prohibits the use of the blood of the beasts offered in sacrifice, he gives this reason for it " because the blood is the atonement:" but when he forbids the use of the blood of the same kind of beasts, when slain at home for common use, he founds the prohibition on a lasting reason, Deut. xii. 20, 21, 22, 23, 24. " for the blood is the life, and thou mayest not eat the " life with the flesh. Thou shalt not eat of it: " thou shalt pour it on the ground like water." Had Israel been allowed to eat the blood of beasts slain for common use, or had the use of such blood been prohibited because it was the atonement, then soon as the blood of beasts ceased to be the atonement, the reason for abstaining from it would have ceased, and so the law itself requiring such abstinence. But Israel was not allowed to eat the blood of any kind of beast for a reason of a moral or perpetual nature, therefore till the blood cease to be the life of the animal no man can eat it, without forfeiting all title to his own life, or right to the blessing annexed to abstinence from blood. This blessing

blessing is very important, Deut. xii. 25. "Thou
" shalt not eat it, that it may go well with thee,
" and with thy children after thee, when thou
" shalt do that which is right in the sight of
" the Lord."

The sum of what has been said on this argument is—The blood of beasts slain in sacrifice was forbid to be eaten, because, for the time then present, it was the atonement. This reason was of a temporary and figurative nature, and must necessarily cease when beasts ceased to be sacrificed. It is impossible for us to break this law now, as no beast can be offered in sacrifice, according to the gospel. But as the law enjoining abstinence from the blood of common animals, or beasts slain at home for ordinary use, is founded upon a reason which is lasting as the earth itself, the law founded on that reason must be obligatory to the end of the world and obligatory on all mankind. For this is the law given to Noah, the father of all nations, in the everlasting covenant for all the earth; in which Jew and Greek, christian and heathen, are all equally interested.

3dly, It is argued, that as the fat was forbidden to be eaten under the law, the argument is equally

equally ſtrong againſt eating the fat as the blood. Let us examine and ſee. 1ſt, The fat was not prohibited in the grant of animal food given to Noah, and in him to all mankind: neither is any ſuch prohibition to be found in the new teſtament, and conſequently it cannot bind the conſciences of chriſtians, who are under the law to Chriſt and not to Moſes. No law of Moſes can bind us but what is taken into the code of laws eſtabliſhed in the new teſtament by Jeſus Chriſt. 2dly, Iſrael were only forbid to eat the fat of the ſacrifices, but were allowed to eat that of the beaſts ſlain for common uſe. We find full directions given with regard to the latter in Deut. xii. 20—26; but not a ſyllable there prohibiting fat, nor any reſervation made of any part of the ſlaughtered animal, ſave the blood only: v. 23, " Only be ſure," in the Hebrew, " be ſtrong that thou eat not the blood." 3dly, Strangers among Iſrael were not forbid to eat the fat, but no toleration was given for them to eat blood.—So deſtitute of foundation is this ſpecious argument. Fat in general was not forbid to be eaten in Moſes law, but none could taſte " any manner of blood"

under

under the higheſt penalties. Proceed we now to the

4th Argument in favours of blood-eating, derived from what our Lord ſays Matt. xv. 11. " Not that which goeth into the mouth defil-" eth a man." It is amazing what influence this weak and wicked argument has had on the minds of men; though evidently framed by the old ſerpent. For 1ſt, The diſtinction between clean and unclean meats was ſtill in full force, when our Lord ſpake theſe words, ſo that no Jew could eat any ſpecies of food, which the law pronounced unclean, but he muſt have been defiled. Had Jeſus himſelf eaten but a bit of ſwines-fleſh, for inſtance, he could not have been our ſaviour. How wicked, then, to put a ſenſe on our Lord's words which even his greateſt enemies never pretended to find in them? 2dly, He explains his meaning in v. 20 " To eat with unwaſhen hands defileth not a " man." He is not ſpeaking of any particular kind of food, but of accidental pollution adhering to food by touching it with foul hands or the like. This cannot defile a man, becauſe " the draught purgeth all meats." 3dly, He means, that eating any kind of food as ſuch cannot defile a foul: but when the heart is confcious that any kind of food is prohibited by God, the wickednefs of the heart in breaking a law of God defiles the man in eating the food. Thus not the food, but the breach of the law of God in eating it, defiles the man. This interpretation confifts with fcripture and common fenfe; whereas the other makes our redeemer fpeak contrary both to law and gofpel; as the gofpel itfelf makes meats offered to idols unclean when eaten from reverence for the idol.

5thly, It is pled, that: " commanding to " abftain from meats, which God has created to " be received with thankfgiving," is a part of the character of antichrift, as defcribed by Paul, 1 Tim. iv. 1—5. This muft be antichriftian; fince " every creature of God is good, and no- " thing to be refufed if it be received with " thankfgiving."—To this I reply, 1ft, the " e- " very creature of God" in v. 4. cannot mean every creature God has made; fince ftones, iron, yea poifonous herbs and animals, are certainly to be refufed if offered as food. The every creature in this verfe, then, muft only comprehend the meats in v. 3. or the " meats which " God has created to be received." But this

cannot

*the Lawfulness of Eating Blood.*

cannot include blood, as it never was created to be received by man, but expressly forbidden to be received at all. 2dly, The meats here meant are the meats which antichrist commands men to abstain from: but these do not include blood, since the eating of blood was first, and is still authorized in the world called christian, by the papal power alone. Thus the Pope has proved himself to be antichrist, by forbidding men to eat meats which God created to be received; and commanding them to eat what God never created for that purpose, but has expressly prohibited it ever since the first grant of animal food to man.

6thly, An argument is taken from what Paul says, Rom. xiv. 2, 3, 4. " One believeth that " he may eat all things; another who is weak, " eateth herbs. Let not him that eateth, de- " spise him that eateth not, &c." Hence, it is pled, that blood may be eaten, since Paul does not condemn him, who believeth that he may eat all things, and so blood. But little doest thou think, O vain man, where this reasoning will lead thee! In the 5th verse, Paul says, " One man esteemeth one day above another; " another esteemeth every day alike: let every
" man

"man be perfuaded in his own mind." Hence, it is inferred, that there is no fabbatifm left to the people of God; or that no regard is due to the firft day of the week above any other day. And doubtlefs this inference is as juftly drawn as the former. But, the truth is, we cannot get at Paul's meaning unlefs we attend carefully to the defign he has in view in this chapter. Some of the believing Jews, who had been educated among a fect, who reckoned it unlawful to eat flefh, lived on herbs only as Adam did; others, of more enlarged ideas, judged it lawful to eat flefh alfo, in virtue of the grant of animal food given to Noah. The all things, then, this latter clafs believe they might eat, evidently mean animal as well as vegetable food. But that blood cannot poffibly be here intended is clear from v. 6. where Paul fays " He " that eateth, eateth to the Lord; for he giveth " God thanks." Now it muft be allowed, that all the churches had received a copy of the decree of the apoftles made at Jerufalem, wherein abftinence from blood-eating is made an exprefs term of difciplefhip among chriftians, and confequently every chriftian knew that blood-eating was totally inconfiftent with his profeffion

sion. This must be admitted even by our blood-eaters, as they allow that this edict of the apostles was binding at least till the time of the destruction of Jerusalem, and so long after the date of this epistle to the Romans. In this case it is absurd to say, that a christian could eat to the Lord or give God thanks for what he well knew the Lord had forbidden him to eat. If he could eat blood to the Lord, he might also commit fornication to the Lord; since both are forbidden by the same authority and in the same edict. How brutish is the reasoning of error!

As to the inference deduced from v. 14. " I am persuaded that there is nothing unclean " of itself, &c." it is of no force. Blood never was called unclean by the law of God, as I have proved before; yet it was never allowed to be eaten. Consequently it cannot follow from this assertion that it is lawful to eat blood.

But it is argued farther in support of blood-eating, that it is said in Rom. xiv. 17. " The " kingdom of God is not meat and drink." *Ans.* 1st, The sense is, the Mosaic distinction of meats is abolished in the kingdom of God. But how can this affect the law prohibiting blood,

blood, which was not classed among meats either clean or unclean? 2dly, According to this reasoning, there is no meat and drink in the kingdom of God. But is it possible that Paul can intend to say so, when he had received of the Lord an institution to be delivered to the churches, and by them to be observed till Christ shall come again, in which meat and drink, bread and wine, are essential parts? Or how is it possible that Paul could say that blood is not forbidden in the kingdom of God, when he himself had joined in framing the decree forbidding it, but a few years before? This would make Paul either a fool or a knave; as does the argument taken from

7thly, 1 Cor. x. 25. "Whatever is sold in "the shambles eat ye making no question for "conscience' sake." To this it is replied, 1st, That we have no evidence that blood was sold in the shambles of antiquity; nor does it appear possible that it could be so in warm climes, where it must have putrified in a few minutes after its extravasation. 2dly, Paul is speaking here concerning flesh slain in sacrifice in the idol-temple, and afterwards exposed to sale in the shambles, as is clear from the context.

But

But what has this to do with blood. 3dly, Suppoſing blood to have been ſold in the ſhambles, if the "whatſoever" in v. 25. includes blood, then the "all things" in v. 23. which Paul ſays are lawful for him, muſt include every action even the moſt wicked. 4thly, He cannot here mean to reverſe the apoſtolic decree prohibiting blood, as even blood-eaters admit the obligation of this edict while Jeruſalem ſtood.

8thly, As the apoſtolic decree recorded Acts xv. ſo expreſsly forbids blood-eating, the abbettors of that practice have ſtrained every nerve to explain it away, and turn it into a temporary expedient, intended only to continue in force till the deſtruction of Jeruſalem. In ſupport of this opinion, it is pretended, that this decree was only made with a view to reconcile the Jews to hold communion with the Gentiles, for ſo, ſay they, James inſinuates in v. 21. where he founds the neceſſity of the decree upon this reaſon "Moſes of old time hath in "every city them that preach him, being read "in the ſynagogues every ſabbath day." This is a groſs miſinterpretation of James' words; and it is aſtoniſhing to find writers of ſo great

and

and shining talents gravely supporting so absurd a fiction. Had they but glanced at the foregoing verse, it is scarce possible that a candid mind could have missed the sense of this. "My sentence is, that we trouble not them who from among the Gentiles are turned to God: but that we *write* to them, that they abstain from pollutions of idols, &c." Here it is evident, that James is not giving the reason of the decree, but the reason for putting it in writing. Let us write the mind of the Holy Spirit concerning the freedom of the Gentiles from the law of Moses, and their obligation to abstain from some moral vices, which they reckon indifferent, such are eating things offered to idols, things strangled and blood with fornication. It is necessary to commit this decision to writing, because, as the law of Moses is read in the synagogue every sabbath, and many Gentile believers attend there; these believers among the Gentiles might not know whether they are bound to keep the law of Moses or not, unless we write this decree and give a copy of it to all the churches, that so all may know upon what foot Gentiles are to be received into the church of Christ, and none may

may impose on them again by telling them that they cannot be saved, except they be circumcised and keep the law of Moses.

But since the idea of the temporary nature of this decree is so warmly supported, and so generally received, it is necessary we should expose its weakness and absurdity a little farther.

1st, If the prohibitions in this edict were to cease with the Jewish state, the things or actions prohibited by them must be of an indifferent nature, otherwise they could not become lawful after the destruction of Jerusalem. Moral evils are such at all times and in all places. Yet it is impossible to call these things indifferent without differing from the spirit of truth, who expresly calls them *necessary things*, v. 28. 29. And we must be hard put to it in supporting an hypothesis, when it cannot be done but at the expence of calling in question the judgment of the unerring spirit. Besides, this idea is inconsistent with the very nature of some of the things forbidden, since idolatry and fornication are allowed to be moral evils.—If it be said, some of them are moral and others indifferent, this is a mere assertion unsupported by evidence. The Holy Spirit makes no such distinction,

tinction, but prohibits them all under the same idea as *necessary* things; and who taught us, then, to call them *indifferent?* Sure none but he, who taught Eve to consider the eating of the tree of knowledge as an indifferent thing. —Again, if it be said, that this decree is called " a burden," and therefore cannot be intended to continue in the christian church, then by the same rule the whole law or yoke of Christ must have also ceased with this decree, since the whole is called a burden Matt. xi. last. 2dly, this hypothesis stands on the absurd idea that these concessions on the part of the Gentiles would have reconciled the judaizers to hold communion with them; whereas sun-shine cannot be more evident than this, that nothing would satisfy the zealots for the mosaic system but the entire subjection of the Gentiles to the whole law. For we are expressly told in this very chapter, (v. 1, 24.) that the tenet they every where inculcated was " except a man be " circumcised, and keep the law of Moses, " he cannot be saved." How absurd, then, is it to imagine, that the apostles intended to patch up a peace between these furious zealots and the Gentile christians, while nothing less than

a

a perfect conformity to the law of Moses, on the part of the Gentiles, could have answered that purpose! Nor did this decree in the least abate the rigor of the terms insisted on by the Judaizers, as long after the date of this decree, we find them as stiff in opposing the liberty of the Gentiles as before, as is evident from the epistles of Paul to the Romans and Galatians: and, indeed, how could so trifling a concession as this, be supposed to effectuate this purpose? He must be a stranger to that uncomplying zeal of religious bigotry, who imagines that the Gentiles, by yeilding to one part of the law enjoining abstinence from things strangled and blood, could obtain fellowship with men, who considered the whole law of Moses as of eternal obligation. Had the apostles conceived any such idea, they were truly bunglers in the art of peace-making: particularly when at the same time they condemn the favourite dogma of the Judaizing party in the most full and express terms, and load the zealots themselves with the odious epithets of troublers of the Gentiles and subverters of souls. A bad plan for moderating their zeal! The truth is, no such idea was entertained by the apostles. They expressly loose the Gentiles from any obligation to keep the law of Moses; and only enjoin them to observe laws which were in force long before the Sinai system had an existence.

3dly, Supposing what James says in v. 21, to be the reason for making this decree, it will by no means follow that the obligation of the decree was temporary, or only intended to continue in force till Jerusalem was destroyed. Had this been intended, James would have said, let us oblige the Gentile converts to abstain from things strangled and from blood, because Moses is preached and read in the temple every sabbath day. In this case, soon as the temple was destroyed, the reason of this prohibition would have ceased: and the Gentiles might have eaten blood, when Moses had none to read him in the temple. But since James says, that the decree is obligatory while Moses has in every city them that preach him, being read in the *Synagogues* every sabbath day; it is clear that this decree is in as much force as ever, since Moses in every city, where the Jews reside, has them that preach and read him in the synagogues, with the utmost punctuality, every sabbath day: and surely we have as much reason, to abstain from giving offence to the Jews as ever.—Thus, if we should even admit the blood-eaters' sense of this text, the inference they deduce from it in favour of blood-eating is wild, absurd and inconclusive.

It is argued farther, that Paul himself makes eating meats offered to idols a matter of indifferency, 1 Cor. x. 25, 26, 27. as he allows christians to eat meats offered to idols, when invited to a feast in an unbeliever's house, making no question for conscience' sake; only in case he was informed that the meat set before him had been offered to idols, he is advised to abstain from it, lest he should offend a weak brother. But this whole argument is founded on a mistranslation of the word Idolothytes, which does not mean meats that has been offered to idols, and afterwards sold in the shambles as common flesh, but idol-sacrifices, all of which were eaten in the temple of the idol: in which case eating Idolothytes was an act of worship performed to the idol in his temple; whereas eating the same flesh when it had been exposed in the shambles as common flesh, could not infer the least veneration for the idol, being eaten as a common thing. Thus Paul condemns eating idolothytes in the ſtrongeſt terms, calling it idolatry and a partaking of the table of devils, v, 14, 21. of this chapter, becauſe it was an explicit act of idol-worſhip: while he permits the believers to eat the ſame fleſh, if ſold in the ſhambles, provided they did not give offence thereby to the weaker brethren. How wicked is it, then, to make Paul contradict himſelf, while he ſpeaks in the moſt clear, accurate and conſiſtent manner!

That eating Idolothytes is an act of everlaſting criminality is clear from Rev. ii. 14—24. There we find the Lord of the churches expreſſing the higheſt indignation againſt the churches of Pergamos and Thyatira becauſe they ſuffered ſome falſe brethren among them to teach the lawfullneſs of eating Idolothytes and of committing fornication. Sure matters of indifferency could not merit ſuch dreadful puniſhment.

I know that it is pleaded, that the prohibition of eating meats offered to idols, whether in the idol-temples, or in private houſes after the meat had been ſold in the ſhambles, goes upon the ſame foot, even ſcandal and offence. In ſupport of this opinion it is alledged, that the apoſtle (1 Cor. viii. 4—end) ſeems to ſuppoſe that

that thefe who have knowledge "that an idol "is nothing in the world, and that there is no "other God but one," and fo can eat without any religious refpect to, or veneration for the idol, might without criminality fit at meat even in the idol's temple, were it not for fear of enfnaring or offending the confciences of weaker chriftians, who have not fuch enlarged degrees of knowledge.—To fet this matter in a clear light it is neceffary to obferve, that Paul is here replying to the arguments of a fet of philofophizing chriftians in the church of Corinth, pretenders to fuperior refinement in idea and fentiment. Of this their liberal knowledge they boaft, ver. 1. "We know that we all "have knowledge." Very well, fays Paul, but what avails knowledge without love? It only puffs up the poffeffor with a vain conceit of himfelf, while only he who loves God is approved of him, v. 1, 2, 3. But with refpect to idol-facrifices what do you know? Why, fay they, we know that an idol is nothing, or is no divinity at all; and confequently in eating meats offered to idols, we eat not with any religious refpect to the idol, but view it as common food, provided for us by the one God and

Father

Father of all. In this case we are not guilty of idol-worship. To this Paul replies,—Every man has not this knowledge; but some weaker christians, imagining that there is some invisible spirit present in the idol, eat it as a sacrifice offered to that spirit, and so defile their consciences with the guilt of idolatry.—But, reply these philosophers, meats in themselves can never recommend us to God, neither by eating them nor by abstaining from eating. True, says Paul, but the circumstances of an action are to be taken into the account. Without entering then at present into the merits of the question, whether it be lawful for men of your liberal ideas to eat the sacrifice of the idol even in his temple, I shall only say, take heed lest by this liberty of yours, you lead a weak brother into idolatry, by emboldening him to partake of the idol-sacrifice, while he is conscious of some respect to the idol as the vehicle of some spirit. Thus by sinning against the brethren, ye sin against Christ.

In this eighth chapter, then, it is evident that Paul reasons against eating Idolothytes only on the foot of scandal and offence, and shews that even in this view no christian could eat them without

without sin. But this does not say that such a practice was not unlawful in itself, or that Paul could produce no other argument against it. So far from this, he resumes the subject in the tenth chapter, where he enters fully into the merits of the cause, and demonstrates the fallacy of the specious arguments produced by the philosophizers in the 8th chapter. There he proves in the strongest light, that eating the sacrifice of any God, whether real or pretended, is an expression of fellowship with that God, and an acknowlegement of his divinity. Thus, v. 7. Israel were guilty of idolatry by eating the sacrifices of Baal-peor, even while they did not offer these sacrifices. Again, in v. 16, 17. he shews that we express our communion or fellowship with Jesus Christ by eating the bread and drinking the cup, which are to our faith the body and blood of Christ our sacrifice. Eating the supper is feasting on the sacrifice of Calvary; and so is the the highest expression of our fellowship with the true God. In the same manner, v. 18. Israel after the flesh, by eating the sacrifice, were partakers of the altar. Hence he concludes from the clearest premises, that eating the idol-sacrifices is the strongest expression

of

of holding communion with the idol, and consequently must be idolatry. "Wherefore, my "dearly beloved, flee from idolatry." Then he proceeds to demonstrate the fallacy of the assertion, that an idol is nothing, and that what is offered to it is no sacrifice, v. 19, 20. True, says he, the statue of wood, stone, &c. is no animated being of any kind in itself, but the Gentiles imagine that some invisible spirit or demon inhabits the statue, and so when they offer sacrifices before the statue or shrine, they sacrifice to demons and not to the true God. In this case, by eating the sacrifice with them, which was always done in the temple, you have fellowship with demons or devils; a practice totally subversive of the profession of christianity, being the most express act of idolatry. "Ye cannot be partakers of the Lords table, "and the table of devils."

From the 23d verse to the end of the chapter, he proceeds to shew two cases in which it is lawful to eat things that have been sacrificed to idols; first, when sold in the public mercat as common meat; secondly, when presented at a common entertainment in a private house, provided the christian guest be not informed that

that it has been offered to idols. In cafe he has been informed of this circumftance, he muft not eat, for the fake of his brother's confcience.

In the above view of Paul's reafoning, it is eafy to fee in what fenfe eating Idolothytes is condemned in the apoftolic decree, and why fuch tremenduous judgments are threatened againft the churches of Pergamos and Thyatira, for fuffering any among them to teach the lawfulnefs of eating fuch facrifices. To eat them in the temple of the idol is idolatry, and fo merits the higheft punifhment. Whereas no fuch charge can be laid againft eating them at a common meal or when bought in the fhambles. Thus Paul fpeaks confiftently with himfelf and with other fcriptures: whereas the common interpretation, making it lawful to partake of the table of devils, provided it give no offence to the brethren, renders Paul's reafoning nugatory, and inconfiftent with other parts of fcripture, yea with common fenfe. On this plan, a chriftian may confcientioufly join in the idolatrous rites of the papifts and pagans, provided he has fenfe to know that the whole is a farce!

Thefe Free-thinkers in the church of Corinth feem to have been much devoted to fenfual gratifications.

tifications. Educated in the school of Venus, who had a temple in that city, the common resort for venereal purposes, they considered whoredom as a matter of indifferency, as well as eating sacrifices in the temple of that idol. Thousands of loose women were maintained in the purlieus of the temple for the use of her adorers, who having ate the sacrifice and sung hymns in honour of the goddess, proceeded to the most direct act of her worship. These practices, so agreeable to appetite, and sanctified by custom, were not easily abandoned. These, however, were the chief objects of the apostolic decree at Jerusalem; hence it became difficult to reconcile these practices with the christian profession. Such christians as determined to continue in such usages applied to philosophy, which furnished them with some maxims very convenient for their purpose. " Meats are for the belly, and the belly for meats;" that is, God has suited the appetite to the enjoyment, and the enjoyment to the appetite; consequently there can be no harm in gratifying any natural appetite, since God has made the one for the other. Such is the maxim refuted by Paul, 1 Cor. vi. 12, 13, &c. A maxim which they

extended

extended not only to Idolothytes but to whoredom. These are the "all things" which they said were lawful; all gratifications of the natural appetite, as is evident from the connexion. In the tenth chapter they apply this maxim to vindicate their eating Idolothytes, and in this sixth chapter, to assert their liberty to commit fornication. The common interpretation puts this maxim, "all things are lawful for me," in the mouth of Paul, to vindicate his right to eat Idolothytes even in the temple of the idol, as an act not criminal in itself, but only so in case of its giving offence to others. If so, by a parity of reasoning, he adopts it in chapter 6th that he may assert his liberty to commit whoredom, as he is speaking of that subject only in that chapter.

The fact is, Paul only takes up these libertine principles that he may confute them. This he does not by opposing authority to them but reasoning and exhortation. "I speak as to "wise men; judge ye what I say." Thus he opposes them, when employed to vindicate eating idol sacrifices in the tenth chapter: thus also when used to subserve the purposes of fornication in chapter vi. Taking it for granted, says he, for the sake of argument, that all things are lawful, yet it is evident that things lawful to be done are not in every case expedient: and with respect to your favourite maxim " meats for the belly, and the belly for meats," this cannot extend to vindicate whoredom. The body is purchased by the Lord, and so ought to be subject to the rules he prescribes for it. Our spirit is already joined to the Lord, so as to be one with him: and although the belly, the seat of appetite, must be destroyed in the grave with the meats which support it, yet the radical principles of the body shall be raised up in shape and qualities like Christ's most glorious body. Thus the body in all its members is made for the Lord, or destined for his service here as instruments of righteousness, and to be conformed to his own body in a coming state. The Lord is also for the body, as the pattern or model is formed for the thing to be formed upon it. He will raise up the body, shape it, and support it by that energy, whereby he is able to subdue all things to himself.

But it is farther argued, that this decree of the apostles is of the same kind with the advice given by James to Paul, recorded in Acts, xxi. 20. 26. viz, that he should take a vow on him,

purify

purify himself and shave his head according to the law; that the believing Jews might see that he walked orderly and kept the law.—Let us compare these two cases and see whether they have any analogy to one another. The apostolic decree was written and a copy of it given to every church, as obligatory upon all: whereas this advice of James to Paul was only given to one man, and he a Jew, while at the same time it is declared not to be binding on the Gentiles at all, v. 25. " As touching the Gentiles who " believe, we have written and concluded, that " they should observe no such thing." By this we are certain it is not a law of Christ, else the believing Gentile must have observed it as well as the Jew. Again, this advice was only to be observed on a particular occasion, and that in Jerusalem only; whereas the decree is declared binding on all christians in every place, and on every occasion. So that it is impossible to find the most distant analogy between the apostolic decree and the advice under review.

It is argued again, that this decree is not a law, as it is given in the form of advice, and not enforced by threatening in case of disobedience. But if this argument be conclusive, we shall

shall scarce find a law of Christ in all the new testament, as by far the greater part of his laws are delivered in the form of exhortations. He says, for instance, to the church in Laodicea "I counsel thee to buy of me gold tried in the "fire, that thou mayest be rich." This is an advice; but will any person say that it is not a law, or that we may reject it with impunity? The truth is, the exhortatory form best suits the genius of the laws of Jesus. Love only can obey them; and love needs no threatenings to terrify it into obedience.

Lastly, The advocates for blood-eating boast that their cause derives a very strong support from the epistles to the churches in Pergamos and Thyatira, Rev. ii. 14—24. These churches, say they, are condemned for suffering some members to teach the lawfulness of committing fornication and eating Idolothytes; but they are not condemned for teaching that things strangled and blood may be lawfully eaten. Whence they conclude, that the obligation of this last part of the apostolic decree had ceased before the date of these epistles, else it would have been mentioned on this occasion. To this I reply, No part of this decree would have been
mentioned

mentioned on this occasion, had not these churches acted contrary to it; nor could these churches be blamed but in so far as they disobeyed the law. Ere this argument, then, can be of use to the blood-eaters, they must prove that these churches taught the servants of Christ to eat things strangled and blood. Could they prove this, their argument would be invincible, as we do not find these churches reproved for these practices. But as we have not the least hint that any in these churches either taught or practised blood-eating, how could the Holy Spirit charge them with crimes, of which they were not guilty? The truth is, motives of animal pleasure might easily seduce men to eat Idolothytes and commit fornication; but it does not appear from any part of the history of the christian church, that in so early a period, or even long after, any person professing christianity had got it into his head to lay himself on a level with dogs, wolves and cannibals by eating blood.

But what puts the matter beyond dispute is, the whole of this decree is rejoined in the most express terms, and declared to be binding on the churches to the end of the world, in the epistle

epistle to the church in Thyatira, Rev. ii. 24, 25. The apostolic decree was called a burden when first made. Alluding to this Christ says " I put upon you no other burden. But that " which you have already, hold fast till I come." Now it will be allowed, that this church must have been possessed of a copy of the decree under review, as a copy of it was sent to every church; nor is there one single article in that decree reversed here, but the whole declared to be in force till Jesus come again.

Thus I have weighed all the arguments, and even the shadows of argument, produced in favour of blood-eating, in the balance of the sanctuary and have found them wanting. I shall only add on this head, that it appears surprizing, that men should have taken so much pains in wresting the scripture to support a practice, so beastly in itself, and so expressly prohibited in the word of the living God. In the sacred records, we no where read of blood being given to any but as a punishment. The blood of Jezebel was given to the dogs as a punishment upon her for her wickedness; and blood is said to be given to the mother of harlots for the same reason, Rev. xvi. 6. " give her
" blood

"blood to drink, becauſe ſhe is worthy—Worthy, as ſhe firſt taught chriſtians to drink the blood of beaſts, and then drunk the blood of ſaints. The blood-eaters may prove, if they can, that in any inſtance blood was given for food to any as a bleſſing.

We ſhall now take a view of the ideas, concerning blood-eating, entertained by the heathens and primitive chriſtians, downward to the ninth century; and then ſee on what occaſion and by what authority, blood-eating came to be introduced among chriſtians, ſo called.

As to the heathens, we have obſerved already, they viewed the ſacrificial blood as ſacred, and ſo proper only to be uſed in drink-offerings to their Gods. With reſpect to common blood, they never ſeem to have conſidered it as food, at leaſt during the period of ſacred hiſtory. The tradition from Noah, their common anceſtor, ſeems in general to have been religiouſly obſerved, in this reſpect: and what is noticeable, according to the ſcripture-idea, they gave blood to criminals, chiefly bulls' blood, to drink, by which they died. In Prideaux's *connections*, we have a variety of inſtances of that kind. Some ſuicides, alſo, put an end to their

their life by the same means. Sometimes, they drunk the blood of their enemies, not as food, but as an expression of their highest indignation against them, and with a view to pierce the hearts of their surviving friends with the most poignant sensations of grief and rage. This was only done, howbeit, on some very particular occasions.

But it imports us more to know what ideas christians entertained on this point, during the first ages of christianity. Nor are we at any loss to obtain full information on this head.

*Justin Martyr*, who became a christian a little more than thirty years after the death of the apostle John, and wrote his dialogue with *Tryphon*, A. D. 151. has these words; "For that "righteous Noah was permitted by God to eat "of every animal, excepting flesh *with the blood*, "which is suffocated or strangled, you have an "account given you by Moses in the book of "Genesis."

*Clemens Alexandrinus*, in his *Pedagogue*, A. D. 193. says "it is not lawful for men to touch "blood." And again, "It is ridiculous to sup- "pose that the saying of St Paul, about what is "sold

"fold in the mercat, is a repeal of the apofto-
"lical canon."

Again, the *apoftolical canons* were written before A. D. 200. and in that book we find it decreed, that "If any bifhop or prefbyter, or deacon, fhall eat flefh with the blood of its life, or that is torn by beafts, or which died of itfelf, let him be deprived: but if it be one of the laity, let him be fufpended from communion."

*Minucius Felix*, in his *Octavius*, written A. D. 213. fays, "But for us Chriftians, as we think it unlawful to be fpectators of your bloody fights, fo cannot we endure to hear of them; and we have fo much averfion to human blood that we do not fo much as tafte of the flefh of beafts, if we know there is any thing of blood in it."

Moreover, *Eufebius* (Ecclef. Hift. B. 5. c. 1.) recites a faying of Biblias the martyr thus: "How fhould perfons eat little children, for whom it is unlawful to eat the blood even of irrational creatures?"

*Tertullian* wrote his *apologetic* before A. D. 200. and from him we have thefe words—"For fhame, therefore, blufh when you meet a Chriftian, who will not endure a drop of
"the

"the blood of any animal among his victuals, and therefore, for fear any should be lodged among the entrails, we abstain from things strangled, and such as die of themselves.— Among other experiments for the discovery of christians, this is one, to present them with blood-puddings, as very well knowing our opinion about the unlawfulness of eating blood. This, I say, is a stumbling block and offence you lay in the way of christians; and what a strange thing is it, that you who know well that the christians are so religiously averse to the blood of beasts, should imagine them so sharp set upon the blood of men?"

From these testimonies of the above quoted venerable writers, we find not only what was the view they themselves had of blood-eating, but the universal opinion of all christians; among whom the perpetual obligation of the apostolic decree against blood-eating was held as an indisputable article of faith. A religious aversion to blood was considered by the heathen, as characteristical of a christian.

I might have adduced a number of other testimonies equally respectable; such as that of

*Origen*

Origen in his book against *Celsus*, written, A. D. 249. of the council of *Gangrena*, and that of *Orleans*, A. D. 538. The sixth general council in *Trullo*, A. D. 683. Nay, even one down in the dark age of Louis the pious, A. D. 816.* All of these concur in establishing the idea of the perpetual obligation of the law against blood-eating.

These things considered, it may be asked with astonishment, By what authority do christians eat blood, and who gave them such authority? To this I reply, by the sole authority of the church of Rome, the mother of harlots and of all the *abominations* of the earth—An authority, which, for many long and dark ages, challenged the obedience of all christendom, and which still, by a secret but powerful influence, enthralls the minds of protestants themselves. Transubstantiation, the monstruous production of the eighth century, nurtured by the care, and supported by the authority of the all-deceiving see, came by degrees to be received into the creed of mankind as an article of divine faith. Meantime, while the many worshipped

* So late as A. D. 976 a body of English canons contains strong injunctions upon all christians to abstain from eating blood.

shipped this unsightly idol, some doubted, calling in question his divine original. These, among other arguments, produced that of the law against eating animal blood. If, said they, the cup in the Lord's supper be filled with the literal or real blood of Jesus Christ, we are forbidden to drink of it, by the law of God prohibiting blood. To get rid of this troublesome argument, the Pope was obliged to change a standing law of God into a temporary expedient; and thus exalting himself above all that is called God, pronounced that lawful, which God has in all ages declared unlawful, and against which he has denounced the most tremenduous threatenings.——Thus blood-eating came into fashion among christians, or rather antichristians. The same authority, which forbade men to eat meats, which God created to be received, commanded them to eat what God has not created to be received at all. This is the sole authority any one has for eating blood. If any man think it a good one let him obey it. Christians know no such authority.

But as God has poured wisdom, goodness and beauty over all his works, I have no idea of a divine law dictated by pure sovereignty or
arbitrary

arbitrary power. The universal Lord is wise and good; and every thing that comes forth from the Lord of Hosts wears obvious traces of wisdom and love. Let us apply this observation to the law before us, that we may see how far it can prove itself the offspring of a wise and benevolent principle.

1st, When love dictates a law, the law must be calculated to promote the happiness of the subject, since love seeketh not her own, but her neighbour's good. Such is the law prohibiting blood. The more minutely philosophy has examined the constituent principles of blood, the more fully is she convinced that it is not only improper, but a dangerous food for man. It is allowed to contain very little nourishment—it is exceedingly subject to putrescency, as daily experience proves. Scarcely is it extravasated and exposed to the air, but it assumes obvious symptoms of putridity. Hence wolves, foxes, &c. more sagacious than human blood-eaters, suck it from the veins of the animal. Expose it a short time to the influence of the air; and the most voracious brute will refuse to taste it.—Finally, blood is the seat and organ of almost every species of animal-disease.

eafe. Inflammation and putridity are the feeds of difeafe: and thefe have not only their origin in the blood, but are often concealed and fecretly working in that fluid, long ere the difeafe itfelf gives vifible fymptoms of its exiftence in the fyftem. Had we juft views of the matter, then, we would not only forbear to eat blood, but we would give God thanks for manifefting his love to us in prohibiting a morfel fo dangerous to the health of man.

2dly, This law is alfo the refult of that wifdom, which fhines in every part of the divine plan, framing the whole in perfect harmony; adapting every thing to every thing. None of the milder animals eat blood: none but the moft ferocious, favage and artful brutes, as wolves, foxes, dogs, live on this aliment. Humanity is the characteriftic of man. How improper, then, would it have been to have commanded or even permitted man to act as a brother to lions, foxes, dogs and wolves, the moft ferocious of the brutal world! Such a law, indeed becomes the papal power, the monfter " drunk " with the blood of the faints;" but it cannot " come forth from the Lord of Hofts, who is " wonderful in council, and good to all."—Again,

gain, God alone is Lord of life: the bestowal and support of it is wholly in his hand. It was certainly proper, then, that this idea should be kept alive in the mind of man by forbidding him the use of blood, which is the life, lest he should forget his dependance on God for so important a blessing. Life is the foundation of all enjoyment. Hence to acknowledge God as the absolute proprietor of life is to own him as the author of all that either sustains or makes it happy.—Finally, the propriety of this law will appear, if we consider, that to partake of the blood is a symbol of our oneness with the creature, of whose blood we partake. We are commanded now to drink the blood of the son of God. Why? Because we are one body with him, living in his life, united to him as members of his body. Now all the members of the same body must have a right to partake of the blood *i. e.* the life of that body. This is finely expressed in the supper of our Lord. There we drink the blood of the son of God, as an expression of our living in his life, and of our being members of his body. In this view, to eat the blood of a brute is a symbol of our union with that brute: an expression of our living its life, as of the same spirit and temper with it. The life, disposition and temper of the animal is not in the flesh but in the blood. Hence there is no impropriety in the law allowing us to eat flesh, which we possess in common with every other animal: but till we be one body and one spirit with the brute, it must be the highest absurdity to live on the brute's life by participating of its blood.

Thus we have seen that the law against blood-eating, founded upon an eternal reason, stands immoveable as the covenant of the day and night, of which it is a part. It is a law of gratitude founded upon a free grant or promise of benefits, which stands firm while the sun and moon endure. None of these promises given in the charter to Noah have failed. The seasons regularly interchange; mankind increase and multiply; vegetable and animal food are still provided; the bow is still seen in the cloud, nor has the earth been again deluged with water, although the imagination of man's heart be evil continually. Nor has God failed to require the blood of our lives at the hand of the shedder: at the hand of every beast, Exod. xxi. 28. at the hand of every man, Deut. xix. 11, 12.

In

In all ages, the blood of the flayer is the ranfom of the life or blood of the flain. Thus the promife has been literally fulfilled. It is alfo myftically accomplifhed, in all the facrifices of divine appointment. While the law ftood, the blood of beafts muft make atonement for our fouls: at the hand of every facrificial beaft he required it; till he, who is "every man's brother," appeared, even Jefus Chrift, at whofe hand the full ranfom of our fouls has been required. By him, too, the firft fhedder of man's blood, even the devil, the murderer from the beginning, has had his blood fhed. This author of murder fhall be deftroyed out of the kingdom of God, by the power of the crofs of Chrift, who came to deftroy him that had the power of death, even the devil.—Thus all the grace, and all the promifes conveyed by this charter ftand for ever: who, then, fhall reverfe the law of gratitude founded upon them?

I have already obferved, That facrifical blood was forbidden to men, becaufe it is the atonement. This law ceafed of itfelf with the Mofaic difpenfation, for a very obvious reafon, as the blood of beafts then ceafed to be the atonement.

ment. So far then, as this law respected the blood of beasts it must have ceased with the reason on which it was founded. The blood of beasts now is wholly common; and is to be abstained from only because it is the life. Yet it must be carefully observed here, that we have still our atonement by the blood of Jesus, and the law prohibiting sacrifical blood, so far as it respects that of Jesus, is still in force. Blood is still the atonement and therefore must be abstained from still.

This assertion may seem liable to objection, since Jesus our atonement says expressly, "Except ye eat the flesh of the son of man, and drink his blood, ye have no life in you." Here he enjoins the drinking of his blood as essentially necessary to our eternal life. Is not this a reversal of the law prohibiting the use of the atoneing blood?—This objection merits particular attention.

To have just ideas of this matter it is necessary to observe, That in the constitution of grace, revealed at the introduction of sin, two kinds of blood were appointed as symbols of the blood of Jesus; namely, the blood of the sacrifical animals, as of bulls and goats, and

and the blood of the grape. Yet though both these were types of the same thing at the bottom, a little closer attention will convince us that they did not prefigure the blood of our sacrifice, in the same respect. The former was a figure of that blood, which Jesus shed on Calvary to make atonement for sin; the blood or life which he received from old Adam, even animal blood, or what we may call the blood of his mortality. This was a blood which he had in common with his brethren of mankind; a life which he could lay down or lose for our sakes. Of this blood that of the sacrifical animals was a just figure; as, 1st, it was shed for the remission of sin; 2dly, shed by the priest; 3dly, atonement was made by it; 4thly, It was poured at the bottom of the altar, as Christ's at the foot of the cross; and, finally, was not to be eaten as if it had been a common thing. From this last circumstance, it is easy to see, that, if it be lawful for us now to drink the blood of Jesus, then the sacrifical blood under the law was not a type of the blood of Jesus at all, as it was expressly forbid to be eaten. Nor is there any way of getting rid of this difficulty, but by observing that we are no where commanded

manded to drink the animal blood of Jesus at all. The law of God has prohibited the drinking of any animal blood whatever, and to drink the blood of Jesus literally, or that blood which run in his animal-veins, were it possible, would be as unlawful and hurtful as to drink the blood of any other animal. We have no occasion for his mortal life: we have it already. He partook of our flesh and blood, that we might partake with him in a far higher species of life; that we might imbibe the life of his immortality.

We may then let them keep the animal blood of our sacrifice, who have it already. The Jews said "Let his blood be upon us and our chil-"dren:" and it is on them according to their wish. The papists drink it in the cup of the mass, and drink judgment to themselves, by trespassing against the express commandment of the Holy Ghost, prohibiting the use of animal blood, in this sense of the blood of our sacrifice, no man can nor dare drink it but he shall be cut off from among the people of God.

But the case was, and still is, very different with respect to the blood of the grape. That it was a symbol of the blood of Jesus is clear

from

from John xv. 1. "I am the true vine," or the truth, of which the vine in its blood was but a shadow. It is so still; as is evident from its use in the supper of our Lord; wherein the wine in the cup is called symbolically, The new testament in his blood, or the blood of the new testament. The blood of the grape however, is not a figure of the mortal life or animal blood of Christ, but of his resurrection-Life, or of that life he was possessed of when quickened by the spirit, after he had been put to death in the flesh. This is a blood or life of immortality, altogether different from the life he derived from the old Adam, as it is not subject to mortality, communicating immortality even to his very body. Now he dieth no more; death hath no more dominion over him.

This is the blood of Jesus, which we drink in the sacred cup of the supper; for it is the blood or cup which he said, (Matt. xxvi. 29,) he would " drink new with his disciples in his " Father's kingdom." That the blood of the vine was a symbol of it, or the vehicle for conveying it, he intimated at the same time, when he calls the life or happiness he now enjoys at the Father's right hand the fruit of the " vine."

The

The cup expressive of his resurrection-life and joy was not filled with the blood of bulls or goats but with the blood of the grape.

This blood of the grape has honours superior to those of the blood of animals. It was given to man even in paradise itself, before sin entered, where it stood as a type of the tree of eternal life, in the midst of the paradise of God. This honour it had before sacrifical blood was a type at all. It was, also, drunk in all the drink-offerings of believers, from the time of the institution of sacrificature, and will continue to be so till Jesus come the second time: whereas the sacrifical blood was never allowed to be drunk at all, because it was the symbol of the mortal life, which had the curse of the law, upon it; of which curse the new man, the believer never shall taste.

The propriety of appointing the blood of the grape, as the symbol of the resurrection-life of Jesus is very striking. Unlike the blood of animals, of all fluids the most subject to putrescency, the blood of the grape is capable of being long preserved from corruption, and is the best antidote to putridity in all the vegetable kingdom. Besides, it conveys life, spirit, vigor,

joy

joy and exhilaration to man, or in the sacred language "wine chears the heart of man," yea of God himself, (Judges. ix. 13.) being used in the drink-offerings of God; whereas every creature, fed by animal blood is gloomy, malignant and joyless. How fine a figure, then, is the blood of the grape of the blood of Christ as raised from the dead to incorruption, light, vigor, joy and immortality!

Of this blood we drink literally in the sacred service of the Lord's Supper. There we really drink the blood of the grape with our mouth, and our faith no less really drinks or imbibes the resurrection-life, joy, strength and immortality of the Son of God, through its instituted symbol and vehicle of conveyance. This is the wine, we drink new with him in his father's kingdom. He, who drinketh not this blood of the Son of God, has no life in him.

This blood of the grape has been used in the same manner, in the sacred services of the church of God, in all ages. It was used in the drink-offerings of the law, and that always after the atonement had been made, by the sacrifice of the burnt-offering or sin-offering: and it is used in the cup of the gospel after the atoneing sacrifice

sacrifice of Jesus, in commemoration of that great event. The drink-offerings of old were always offered in the faith of remission of sin and a right to life, obtained by the atonement previously made: and do we not still drink the cup of the new testament in the faith of the remission of our sins, and of our title to life eternal, through the atonement in the sacrifice of Jesus? This is truly the cup of blessing: it is to believers the communion of the blood of Christ! This is the blood of which christians partake by divine authority; while they leave the blood of beasts to beasts and the " worship-" pers of the beast"—that beast, who has totally changed the law of God concerning blood; commanding christians to eat the blood of beasts, which God prohibited; and forbidding them the cup of the blood of the new testament, of which Christ said to his disciples " drink ye all " of it."

## FINIS.

www.ingramcontent.com/pod-product-compliance
Lightning Source LLC
Chambersburg PA
CBHW032226230426
43666CB00033B/1603